The Tennis Experience

Clark Graebner

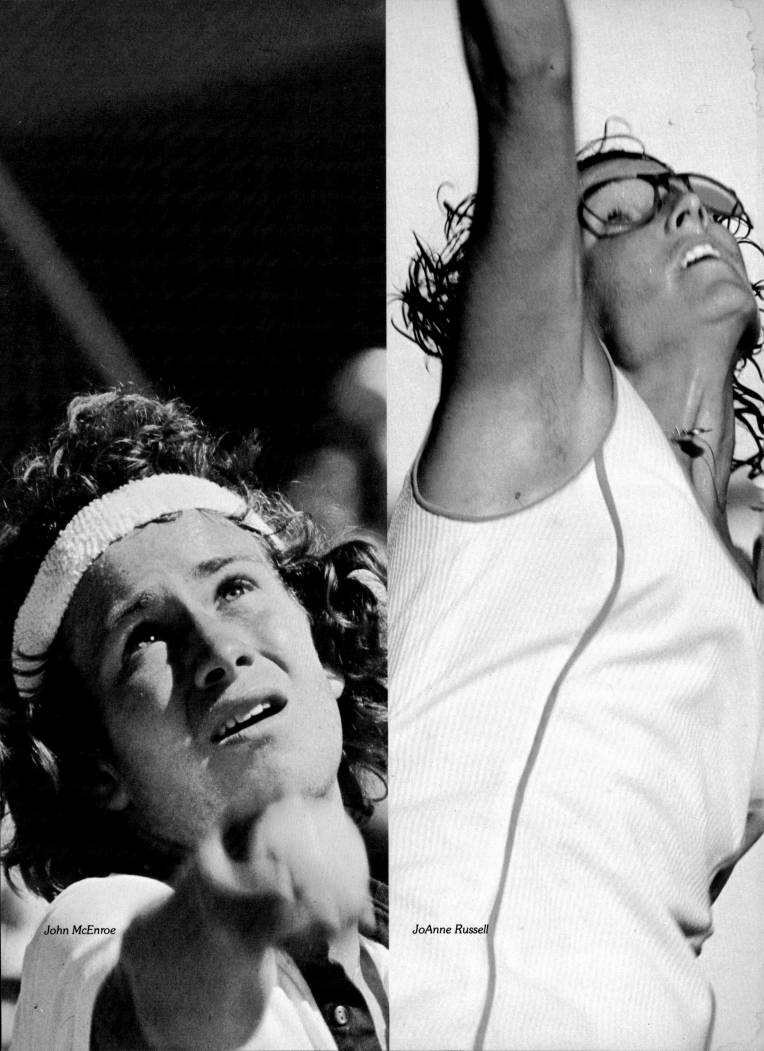

John McEnroe

JoAnne Russell

Renee Richards

Beatrix Klein

The Tennis

Experience

Photography by Melchior DiGiacomo

Text by Eugene L. Scott

A Rutledge Book | *Larousse & Co., Inc.*   *New York, New York 1979*

Ilie Nastase

Caroline Stoll

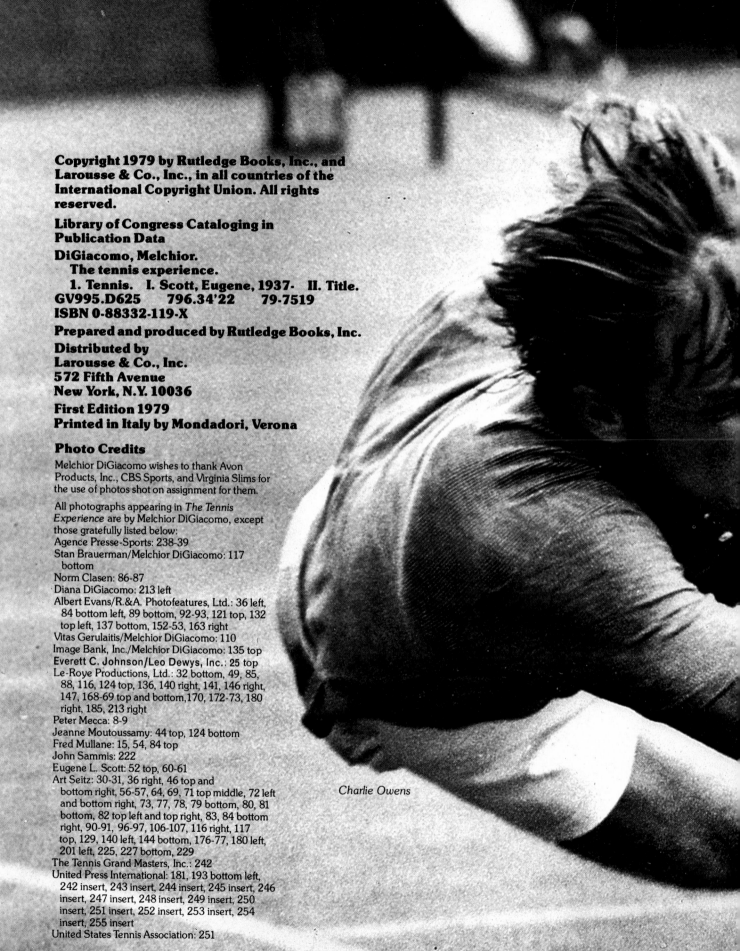

Library of Congress Cataloging in Publication Data

DiGiacomo, Melchior.
   The tennis experience.
     1. Tennis.   I. Scott, Eugene, 1937-   II. Title.
GV995.D625   796.34'22   79-7519
ISBN 0-88332-119-X

Prepared and produced by Rutledge Books, Inc.

**Distributed by
Larousse & Co., Inc.
572 Fifth Avenue
New York, N.Y. 10036**

**First Edition 1979
Printed in Italy by Mondadori, Verona**

Photo Credits

Melchior DiGiacomo wishes to thank Avon Products, Inc., CBS Sports, and Virginia Slims for the use of photos shot on assignment for them.

All photographs appearing in *The Tennis Experience* are by Melchior DiGiacomo, except those gratefully listed below:
Agence Presse-Sports: 238-39
Stan Brauerman/Melchior DiGiacomo: 117 bottom
Norm Clasen: 86-87
Diana DiGiacomo: 213 left
Albert Evans/R.&A. Photofeatures, Ltd.: 36 left, 84 bottom left, 89 bottom, 92-93, 121 top, 132 top left, 137 bottom, 152-53, 163 right
Vitas Gerulaitis/Melchior DiGiacomo: 110
Image Bank, Inc./Melchior DiGiacomo: 135 top
Everett C. Johnson/Leo Dewys, Inc.: 25 top
Le-Roye Productions, Ltd.: 32 bottom, 49, 85, 88, 116, 124 top, 136, 140 right, 141, 146 right, 147, 168-69 top and bottom, 170, 172-73, 180 right, 185, 213 right
Peter Mecca: 8-9
Jeanne Moutoussamy: 44 top, 124 bottom
Fred Mullane: 15, 54, 84 top
John Sammis: 222
Eugene L. Scott: 52 top, 60-61
Art Seitz: 30-31, 36 right, 46 top and bottom right, 56-57, 64, 69, 71 top middle, 72 left and bottom right, 73, 77, 78, 79 bottom, 80, 81 bottom, 82 top left and top right, 83, 84 bottom right, 90-91, 96-97, 106-107, 116 right, 117 top, 129, 140 left, 144 bottom, 176-77, 180 left, 201 left, 225, 227 bottom, 229
The Tennis Grand Masters, Inc.: 242
United Press International: 181, 193 bottom left, 242 insert, 243 insert, 244 insert, 245 insert, 246 insert, 247 insert, 248 insert, 249 insert, 250 insert, 251 insert, 252 insert, 253 insert, 254 insert, 255 insert
United States Tennis Association: 251

Charlie Owens

Forest Hills stadium

Stan Smith

Martina Navratilova

The Warm-Up

For some, tennis is stiff muscles, sweat, and calluses. For others, the sport is ballet—all grace and precision, not a motion out of sync. Somewhere in between lies the truth, for tennis is both poetic and prosaic, and for those who interpret it as entirely one or the other, defeat, whether by artist or artisan, will always manage to strike the proper balance.

The Tennis Experience strives for just such a balance—to capture through original photographs and text the many facets of this game, regarded as simply play or deadly serious business—or both—by galleries and players worldwide. Seen through sympathetic eyes widened by the expertise and imagination of true tennis lovers, this is an engaging look at tennis that is both insightful and spectacular. It focuses on who plays the game—from the beginners' first practice drills, to the superstars' supercharged will to stay on top, to the seniors' mellowed zeal, despite the limitations imposed by years. It showcases the spectacles themselves—Wimbledon, Forest Hills, the new U.S. Open, the French and Italian Championships—and what comprises a tennis life, on and off court.

The Tennis Experience portrays the strength, pain, grace, and speed that form Bjorn Borg's backhand, the concentration of Chris Evert, or the antics of Jimmy Connors and make them all recognizable as part of the same exercise. Perhaps seeing these players in action offers clues to their genius. Throughout, they are shown as people doing something for which they are paid, but for which they must constantly train and practice and to which they must dedicate themselves.

The Tennis Experience also presents the tour—the tedium of the road, the events that attract the pros, the media, and the fans who come to share moments with their favorite players. It previews some who are coming up and it highlights yesterday's heroes—like Billie Jean King, Arthur Ashe, or John Newcombe—who continue to have their days, but not as often, and the seniors of the game, who lend credence to the adage, "We're only getting better."

With the warm-up completed—muscles loosened, minds stretched—*The Tennis Experience* can properly take the court.

1

Vitas Gerulaitis, Sr.

The Beginning

It helps if papa—or mama—is a pro. Lessons are free. You'll be given more time and attention than any of their other customers. And you can ask questions about your grip or footwork any time of the day or night.

A teaching-pro parent pushes a child as far and as fast as the youngster's ability and inclination allow. If the chemistry is right, as in the case of Jimmy Connors and his mother Gloria, a superstar is born. Even if the genetic mix goes sour, the son or daughter will still develop into a better tennis player than 99 percent of the rest of the world's sons and daughters. The reason is simple. Tennis is a discouraging game for beginners. A youngster playing for the first time finds it impossible to accomplish the sport's purpose—to rally. Beginners become frustrated spending most of their initial court time retrieving and picking up balls. It may take a year or more to learn how to effectively keep the ball in play.

The new whiz-bang sport, racquetball, can by comparison be enjoyed instantly. There is no net and no out of bounds—even the ceiling is fair play—and, most importantly, there is no trotting to the fence to fetch the ball. Tennis loses many of its novices to frustration at not being able to get the hang of it quickly. Having a parent as a teacher assures a child of getting past the anxiety barrier. Having a pro-parent also means that more time is spent on practice, that equipment is more readily available, and that there is seldom a hassle getting a court—three ingredients that habitually foil beginners.

Ironically, when speaking of parents as professionals, the reference is not to star players and their children. To date there is no parent-child combination where both have attained world-class stature—although history hasn't lacked for material. Wimbledon champion Sidney Wood, Jr., came close, nurturing Sidney III, a fine college prospect at Yale who was killed in a tragic auto accident during his senior year. Frank Shields, the fabulous-playing and -looking Davis Cupper in the 1930s, had two sons who played tennis, but not exceptionally. Bill Talbert, the famed Davis Cup captain and doubles player, sired two fine athletes in Peter and Pike, but neither had a passion for professional tennis. Neither do Sam Giammalva and his son Tony combine to form an all-star billing. And Francis Gonzalez knows he can stand only in Pancho's giant shadow.

The most successful parent-child coaching relationship seems to occur when the parent is not a superstar. The goal of becoming champion is more pressing to the parent who aspired to the "big time" but never made it. It is as if the coach is trying to springboard the child into a career that the parent never had.

There are many parents who as good players themselves can provide the right environment for total immersion into tennis. Julius and Gladys Heldman, both once modestly ranked players, gave daughter Julie, a Wightman Cup standout for the United States in the 1970s, a sound foundation in stroking fundamentals and afterward encouraged her to seek her own level of excellence. Alex Mayer, an excellent teaching pro in New Jersey, gave his two sons Gene and Sandy a firmer push, but with equally effective results. And of course Vitas Gerulaitis, Sr., once a champion in Lithuania, spent hours with both Vitas, Jr., and Ruta in their formative years. This is a luxury most beginners, and future champions for that matter, don't enjoy—a father who has only two pupils and hits practice balls until his pupils drop with exhaustion.

Few coaches spend all their energies developing a single champion. Most who make a living from teaching dilute their attention among as many as 60 students, both youngsters and adults, concentrating on two or three of the most gifted. The beginner with a parent coach—or sometimes a brother or sister who performs the same function—watching over the education and training of a prospective champion has an incredible edge over the child fending for himself for practice time, tournament scheduling, equipment needs, and overall training regimen.

Connors, Gerulaitis, Chris Evert, Nancy and

Cliff Richey, Pam Teeguarden, Charlie Pasarell, Dick Stockton, Harold Solomon, Marty Riessen, Peter Fleming, and Tracy Austin are just a few of the ranking touring pros who benefited from coaching and coaxing parents.

The parental push is not always healthy. In fact, it can destroy a youngster's will. Unruly parents standing on the sidelines disputing umpires' calls are commonplace at junior tournaments. And they usually don't stop their badgering at courtside. They often spend hours complaining to committee members about the unfair ranking given to their children. But the juniors themselves, embarrassed by their parents' behavior, probably would rather be left alone to fight their own battles, on court and off.

Occasionally households are thrown into total disarray to accommodate junior's practice schedule. While other brothers and sisters are ignored, junior is chauffeured from tournament to tournament without regard for equal family time and expense. Obviously parents are invaluable advisors during their children's development, but when you see a proud father attending every match his child plays, chances are he's a super-pushy tennis parent. Ironically, when the child is old enough to choose for himself, he frequently quits in disgust. And, if he doesn't quit, perhaps he should. Too often the tedium and frustration from endless hours of practice and nagging erupts in wild tantrums on court.

Of course poor behavior can be blamed partially on the absurd example the pros set. Tournament directors are not quick to discipline the game's superstars. It is easy to suspend lesser-known players because their absence does not affect gate receipts. But a promoter faces spectator uprisal if Ilie Nastase, Vitas Gerulaitis, or John McEnroe is banned from his tournament. Consequently, the roguish conduct of some of the biggest box-office attractions continues for all to imitate.

Antics or not, becoming proficient enough to "hold your own" is the beginner's first ambition. And there are four important devices that are essential to the development of any beginner: the backboard, the tennis camp, the two-on-one drill, and the tournament.

For 100 years the backboard has been a traditional teaching tool. Until recently, improvements in stroking have been hindered by a lack of court facilities and difficulty in finding partners to practice with. The tennis boom has solved both problems,

but the backboard remains a staple for instruction. Tennis's answer to the golfer's practice tee, the backboard, can be used any time without having to reserve a court or find a willing opponent. And it's free.

Tennis is a game whose strokes must be practiced in countless repetition, and even for experts the backboard is often the simplest means for learning a new shot or changing an old one. Not many players want to be on the receiving end of an opponent trying out top spin for the first time—one person hitting, the other chasing the ball into the woods. A backboard doesn't talk back and needs no apology for mishit balls.

The usefulness of the backboard is being replaced somewhat by the automatic ball machine, which can be placed either on the court or in a "teaching lane," and spits 100 balls at varying speeds and spins in under five minutes. Its use will undoubtedly expand, for ball projection from the machine is infinitely more authentic than a ball rebounded off a wall, and some shots cannot be practiced on a backboard—for example, the top-spin lob or the drop shot. Nonetheless, the backboard, because of its simplicity and economy, will probably never become obsolete, but will remain an indispensable part of the sport's practice aids.

The tennis camp has become an institution not only for youngsters but adults as well. The concept is sound: two or more weeks of intensive instruction with no distractions. The specific teaching techniques employed in each camp are not crucial to the experience. What is important is the environment—total tennis—which is intended to be the catalyst for the player getting forever turned on to the sport. The camp is a focal point for development, both in terms of reward for year-long improvement and as an authentic report card on progress. The most useful aspect of the tennis-camp education is that it quickly lets pupils know how far they really want to pursue their own games.

The routine during a stay at a tennis camp is remarkably standard:

A.M. 8:00 Wake-up call
8:00-8:30 Calisthenics
8:30-9:00 Breakfast
9:15-10:30 Stroking drills
10:30-10:40 Orange juice break
10:40-12:00 Serve and volley practice
P.M. 12:00-12:45 Lunch

1:30-3:30	Organized singles and doubles play
3:30-3:40	Apple juice break
3:40-5:00	Tournaments
6:30	Dinner
Evening	Free playing time

The student never plays so much tennis in such concentrated doses, and the sport with all its weaknesses and strengths is exposed in its most raw and unglamorous form. It is difficult to think of tennis as a purely graceful art form when your feet and hands ache from the blisters of playing six hours a day for a week.

Because most tennis practice consists of playing against a single opponent, practice is usually little more than a warm-up session. To improve passing shots, for instance, the player obviously must learn to "hit 'em where they ain't." But, aiming for winners in the warm-up means there'll be no rallies and consequently no warm-up. What there may be is one irritated opponent.

The two-on-one drill, the most popular instruction technique for advanced players, solves the problem. It positions two players on one side of the court and the practicer on the other, where he can hit from remote angles without exhausting the players opposite. Two people can cover half a court with ease. This exercise is especially good for conditioning because the single player must scramble all over his side to retrieve the ball and punch out individual patterns. After three or four minutes of not missing a shot, the practicer will be ready to switch sides and give someone else a chance.

Of all practice aids, the tournament is the most important. Whether it is a club championship, a public parks knockout, a resort consolation, a 12-and-under event, or the U.S. Open, the competitive elements are the same. The winner must survive multiple rounds of increasingly tough competition to win a silver spoon or a $100,000 purse. One poor performance means elimination.

Training and preparation then must be on two levels—for a single match and for the entire tournament. Countless players have scored a sensational upset one day and lost to a lesser foe the next day—all because they suffered exhaustion or a psychological letdown.

The pressures are monumental. The structure of the tournament is such that there can be no bad days, no letup, or else defeat comes quickly, with no deference to past performance. A player gets one chance to deal with an adversary; no one shares responsibility for defeat. In team sports, victory or defeat belongs to no one person. In golf, the challenge is the course; there is no person-to-person confrontation. The tennis tournament is brutal in its isolation, but total in its triumph or despair.

The magic phrase "junior development," which is bandied about internationally to demonstrate the positive efforts of tennis associations everywhere, is comprised of tournaments and local clinics and instruction, with tournaments receiving the primary emphasis. The exhibitions and clinics funded by regional tennis associations are important for their showcase value, but it is within the private instruction and tournament structure that true training takes place.

The United States, French, and British tennis associations properly take credit for the framework in which their country's tournaments exist. For instance, the United States Tennis Association (USTA) provides a system for ranking over a thousand players nationally and another seven thousand players sectionally in over fifty-seven categories. The lure of a ranking itself brings everyone from juniors to Super Seniors to the tournament circuit. The more tournaments they compete in the better their chances of a higher rank.

The USTA lends its formal blessing to almost ten thousand tournaments every year. But this number does not include the many private-club events, which bring the final count to close to twenty thousand competitions annually. Any player can find a tournament especially suited to his expertise. In fact there are even national novice events for players who have never before participated in sanctioned tournaments.

It used to be that there were isolated breeding grounds for young tennis players. Australia, California, and Florida were the traditional areas that spawned a majority of the world's top professionals. That has changed. Exotic indoor facilities have made it possible for future champions to emerge from virtually anywhere. However, once a talented athlete has been discovered, he or she must be nurtured properly. Junior tournaments in the United States assure enough competition for every player to progress as far as his or her ability permits. Facilities in England and France are more limited, but the best young athletes are always picked early to be part of a national junior team, with free coaching and court time the ever-present incentive.

In the United States the junior Davis Cup, junior Wightman Cup, and the junior Federation Cup teams are advanced training grounds for the young elite. For the late-bloomer, the national 21-and-under tour is an intermediate stepping-stone from the junior ranks to the pro tour. But by far the largest farm system for young players is the intercollegiate tennis program. Over 500 colleges and universities offer scholarships to promising tennis players. With the average cost of a college education currently at about $5000 per year, the carrot for developing one's tennis skills is not limited to those few athletes who dream of becoming another Bjorn Borg. Indeed, the only dilemma is for those few fabulous collegians who are so good that they must weigh the chance of earning enough on the pro tour to more than pay for their own education. Vitas Gerulaitis, Jimmy Connors, and John McEnroe are three young men who quit college after their freshman years to follow the rich rainbow of the pro tour.

While years ago tennis was largely the domain of exclusive club members, it has increasingly become a sport for everyone. Its appeal, however, is not as broadly based for beginners as the game's publicists would have us believe. Equipment has become expensive ($70 for a racket, $20 for sneakers, and $40 for a tennis shirt, not to mention $3 for a tin of balls every time out). Court time, club dues, or park permits further add to the cost. So, although tennis is no longer the domain of the aristocracy, it remains a game for the somewhat affluent. There are junior programs for inner-city youth in America, but these affect only modest numbers when compared to the 35 million Americans playing tennis.

Two questions are asked more frequently than any others about beginner tennis. The first is, "When should I start my child playing?" The answer could be difficult. Of the top 10 players in the world, each started playing at a different age, ranging from 3 to 14 years old. Not much to be learned there except that they were all young—and the trend will continue getting younger. The rigors of constant competition mean that the athletes will start training sooner to take advantage of the body's most supple years, and perhaps burn themselves out earlier as a result.

The "sage" coaches insist there is no single "right" age to start a daughter or son. What does seem to be a common denominator is their advice not to accelerate a child too quickly, else he exhausts real desire before his game matures. A parent should try to make tennis facilities available and to expose youngsters to the sport at the earliest age they show aptitude and interest. Feed that interest and aptitude in measures appropriate to their growth. Don't push, or the child may be shoved away from tennis rather than closer to it.

The second question is part of the first: "Should juniors have lessons right away, and if so, how many?" The rule of thumb is not to spoil the child by arranging a lesson whenever he wants one. It is important for the beginner to be serious enough about tennis to want to practice on his own. It's a luxury to play with the pro, and juniors should show they deserve the session by playing at least 10 times without the pro for every time with him.

Beginners in tennis come in all ages and inclinations. Surely teenagers fill most of the ranks of the first-time players. But, it is never too late to start playing. Certainly if someone is 40 pounds overweight and hasn't exercised for 20 years, preparation time needed to get in shape before starting to play might be discouraging. And most adults won't spend the time to prepare because they don't have it.

Time, however, is the young beginner's greatest ally. Never in their lifetimes will teenagers have as much idle time to learn and practice their sport—all day if they like, and the next day too. They should make the most of it.

Time, on the other hand, is the senior's enemy. He rarely can take enough time from business or other commitments to do pre-tennis exercises, to warm up sufficiently, and to practice. But a 40-year-old novice who takes up tennis has one advantage over his younger counterparts. He will learn the game and its subtleties more quickly; seniors have to—they don't have the patience—or the time—to be beginners for very long.

Getting grips and things together.

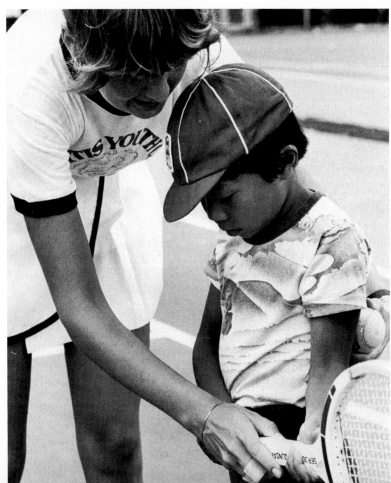

*Group instruction
numbers
from 2 to 200 . . .*

27

. . . *but sooner or later you learn by yourself.*

An extension of the "two-on-one" drill is the "three- and sometimes four- and five-on-one drill" that is practical for group instruction.

Stan Smith

Ian Crookenden, Curtain Bluff, Antigua

32

Tennis is a personal expression of youth . . .

Blaine Willenborg

*. . . an individual style that is
as distinctive as a fingerprint.*

Paul Heath

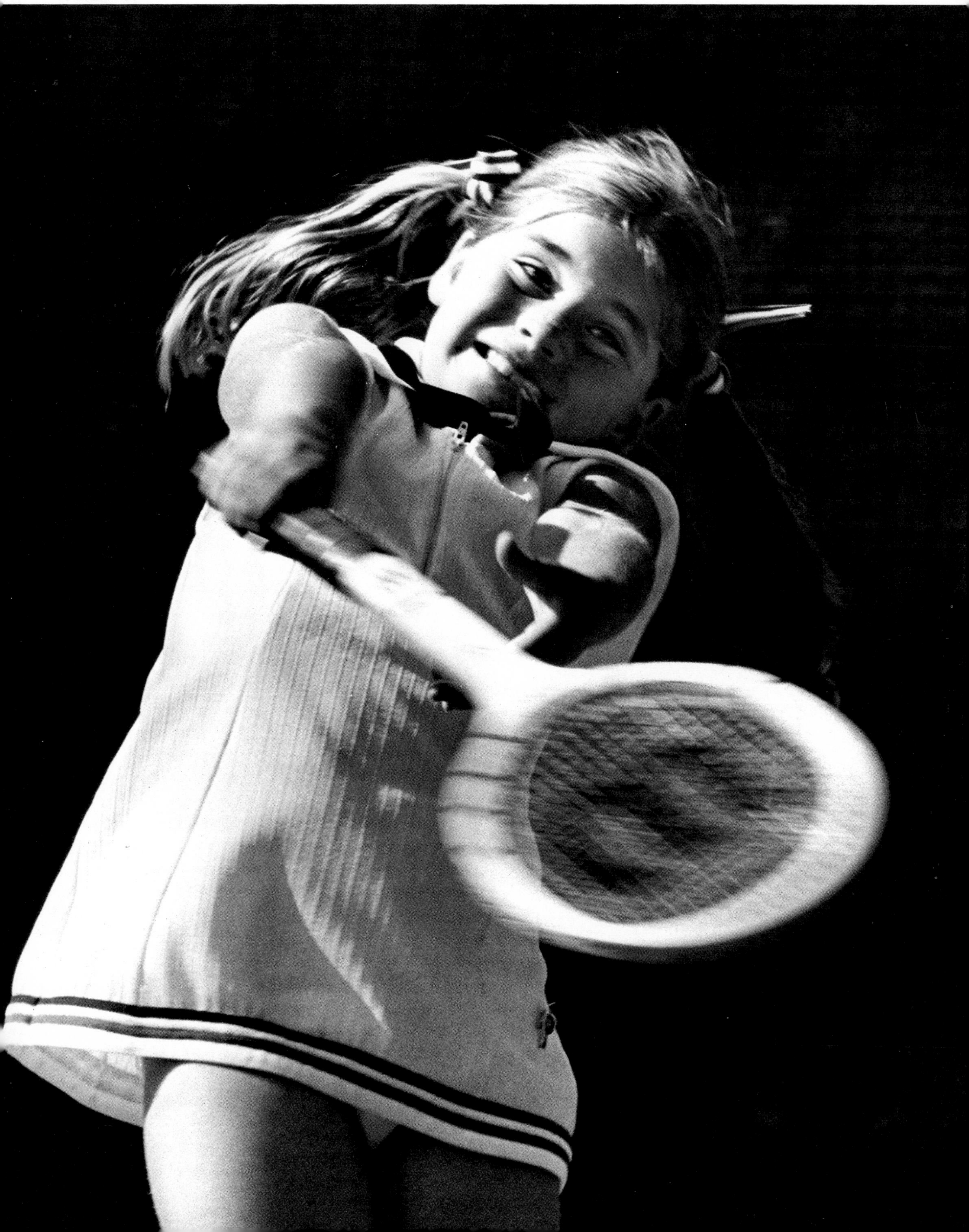

Tony Trabert

Springs for the top eight finishers. The fact that all sponsors—no matter how giant—are like meteors that infuse energy and light (and money) into tennis before disappearing has been given further credence by the report that Colgate will abandon tennis sponsorship after 1979.

The women pros are extraordinarily well organized; they have no competing tours. If Evert, Austin, and Navratilova decide to play in February, they have only one tournament choice (compared with the international smorgasbord of the men's schedule). This may be accidental or the result of a hardheaded strategy not to scatter the thin ranks of the great lady pros more than spectators or sponsors will tolerate. Whereas the men's superstars may spread themselves over three different tournaments (and continents) in one week, if Evert is not entered in a women's draw, sponsors and spectators feel slighted.

As consolidated as the women are, there is no great sense of tradition in their tour, even though its trappings are similar to the men's. What Avon backs was born only nine years ago, and it doesn't help anyone's sense of continuity that Virginia Slims is no longer part of the circuit it spawned.

In addition, the women's tournaments are played largely indoors in arenas that have no traditional association with tennis. Of course the women separated themselves from the classic outdoor setting of tennis when they joined World Team Tennis en masse in 1974. Suddenly there were no women stars to play the summer circuit. Cincinnati, Indianapolis, Toronto, and Orange were stripped of the best drawing cards, but since WTT barely skimmed major talent from the men's ranks, their summer Grand Prix grew stronger.

The women are caught in the middle, with WTT collapsing and no traditional sites to turn to. Wimbledon and the U.S. Open remain the critical showcases for the glittering talents of Evert, Navratilova, Austin, Shriver, and the new group of raw talent being developed by the Avon Futures farm system.

Meanwhile, the backbone of the men's tour is the time-honored outdoor 32-, 64-, or 128-player draw that brings players and spectators year after year to cities like Monte Carlo, Düsseldorf, Milan, Louisville, Houston, Melbourne, Bombay, and Hong Kong. Whatever the city, the tournaments provide unique entertainment. Tennis Week is observed with the same attention given to the American Fourth of July weekend. It is a celebration open to everyone.

All week a tapestry of victories and defeats is woven into the draw until on Sunday the narrative is complete—full of frustrations, upsets, drama, and the ultimate triumph of a single athlete.

It is possible for a spectator to miss points in a match and even entire games from distractions of conversation, cocktails, or both, without losing the sense of the event. A tournament is more than an assortment of points and games, it is essentially an experience. That experience includes sensing the unique mix of players—a doubles pairing of Tom Okker and Ismael El Shafei is judged by how well they return serve, not that one is a Jew, the other an Arab. That experience is knowing that the players' first act upon arriving at a tournament is to check the draw sheet—will they have a fairly easy path to the quarters or have they drawn an opponent they have lost to three of their last four meetings? That experience means understanding that a fan's adoration of a particular professional may have nothing to do with the player's ranking. Or that a pro's constant companion is idle time—the endless wait until the next match.

What makes a tournament important? Certainly not prize money alone, or an Arab shiek could creat a petromillion-dollar spectacle that would overshadow the U.S. Open. And not just top-name players, or the talent-rich specials like the Pepsi Grand Slam (the top four players in the world) or the Dallas final (top eight players) would be revered as mightily as Wimbledon. Only an electric combination of elements can propel a tournament from ordinary to almost sacred stature. Tradition and history are vital ingredients. No tennis event has become extraordinary in just a year, or even ten years. Wimbledon is over a hundred years old, and the U.S. Championship is almost eighty. When a competition returns with such regularity, fans remember to plan their vacations and social schedules around it. Once formed, spectator habits are difficult to alter and guarantee a base of support year after year.

Of course the national press is a symbiotic part of a tournament's stature; newspaper and television coverage is the tour's life blood. Its presence assures an event's recognition, its absence often signals a quick passage to oblivion.

The U.S. Open is perhaps the best example of

the potent mix of ingredients that forms the tournament experience. Each element—prize money, players, tradition, media arousal, sponsorships, and giant galleries—feeds upon the other, increasing the total energy with an excitement that spills over into less glamorous sectors of the game.

The men's tour is no longer a single entity, but a galaxy of individual constellations, each with separate seasons and properties. The Colgate Grand Prix Masters, an event for the eight top players in the year-long Grand Prix, is the last tournament of the year, even though it doesn't come until the second week in January. Indeed, the tour never ends, but is a continuum of play. The months from January to May are supposedly the domain of World Championship Tennis as a result of a settlement of lawsuits and squabbling between Lamar Hunt's WCT and international amateur forces (the ITF). There has been a gradual erosion of Hunt's exclusivity in this time frame, with independent tournaments being scattered throughout the winter in Denver, Washington, Virginia Beach, Palm Springs, and Las Vegas. The first quarter is even more crowded with the emergence of three team competitions: the World Cup (United States versus Australia), the Marlboro Cup (Europe versus South America), and the Nations Cup (an abbreviated Davis Cup).

There are three important tournaments during this early period. Palm Springs and Las Vegas are official ATP fixtures, but deduct hefty percentages of each player's prize money for the union's operating expenses. Purses approach an ostentatious $300,000 each, an amount almost equaling the total money offered the first year of Open tennis.

But the jewel of the early season is the Dallas final in May. It includes the eight highest finishers of the WCT winter series, and most of the current men's stars—Ashe, Rosewall, Smith, Borg, Connors, Newcombe, and Gerulaitis—have won the $100,000 first prize. Once this was tennis's top purse, but it is in danger of becoming a prosaic offering, so gaudy are the modern game's riches.

The German Championships in mid-May signal the start of the outdoor season in Europe, often played in more darkness and rain than summer sun. The Italian Championships follow, still qualifying as a major title despite the fact players feel like Christians facing hungry and partisan gladiators in the statue-trellised Foro Italico.

The French Championships frame Paris perfectly in flowers and June sunshine. However, only the bravest and most versatile come to compete in the French because of its format—the best of five sets on slow brown clay. It is the game's most severe test. And when it is over, it is on to the English grass. The season begins at Surbiton, Nottingham, Queens, and culminates, of course, at the grandpa of all tournaments, Wimbledon, the last week in June and the first week in July. It is a tribute to the reverence for the Championships, as Wimbledon is so pompously described, that it is allowed two weeks to finish in a calendar already crammed with three and four events each week. Wimbledon, which schedules no matches on either Sunday, is isolated like a religious fortnight; no tournaments compete with it.

Immediately after Wimbledon, players scatter all over the globe. First Forest Hills, a new event with $300,000 in prize money for 16 players and an ABC television contract to soothe the grief of old-timers whose U.S. Open was suddenly moved a few miles away to Flushing Meadow, New York. The same week Grand Prix in Newport and Gstaad compete for a field with the European-zone Davis Cup semifinal. All are on clay except for Newport, which is the sole survivor of an all-grass circuit of a decade ago. In North America, Washington, Louisville, Columbus, South Orange, North Conway, Indianapolis, Toronto, and Cincinnati complete the summer circuit like individual diamonds in a necklace, each sparkling brightly as its week in the sun arrives.

These great tournaments are simply foreplay to the U.S. Open, enshrined in its new stadium—a monument to all in sport that is automated, glittery, and mass produced.

In tennis, the U.S. Open and Wimbledon are the most important tournaments in the world. They share top billing. Other events produce gallant champions and high drama, but the Open and Wimbledon are the giant emblems in the sport's fabric, with all other tennis merely trimming. To an American player, winning the U.S. Open is more cherished than the English title. European players obviously feel the same about Wimbledon. But since most of the sport's sponsorship originates in America, a win on her courts can be converted to plusher endorsements than anywhere else in the world.

After the Open, there is a letdown. Ten years ago Forest Hills signaled the formal end of the season, with only the Los Angeles and San Francisco events providing postscripts. Today the game simply gathers its second wind and procedes on to the final quarter. The ATP World of Doubles in Texas follows the Open in the second week in September, and like most other things in Texas it is a man-made event. No history, but barrels of prize money and an array of tired doubles tandems. Los Angeles, San Francisco, and Hawaii end the U.S. summer Grand Prix, then the tour splits itself and goes to Asia and Europe with isolated extravaganzas in South Africa and Argentina. Finally, Australia, the land of upside-down seasons, starts its state circuit in November while the northern world prepares for winter. The Australian circuit concludes with the Aussie Open, which used to begin the tour but now ends it, emphasizing perhaps that the tour really never opens or closes, but is a single season of tennis that carries on and on . . . .

Any tennis event takes extraordinary organization and foresight to bring all the individual elements together to complete the spectacle. The promotion of a professional event is similar to a giant theatrical production, but with some frightening differences. For instance, the prospect of rain hangs over a tournament director with nightmarish persistence.

A tournament can be in perfect pitch with Connors, Vilas, and Borg in the field, a fat contract for sponsorship in the fold, and a television deal confirmed—and suddenly a thunderstorm strikes during the finals. Dreams turn to mush before one's eyes. Since the tour moves on the next day, postponement is rarely an option. Only Wimbledon has the guts—some say the gall—to offer neither refunds nor rain checks if a downpour cancels a day's play. And rain in England is not unpredictable. Everywhere else in the world promoters do fiscal handstands to try to deal with weather, taking out rain insurance, buying expensive tarpaulins to cover the main courts, moving matches indoors (which also means moving fans indoors, a logistical catastrophe in itself), mopping up courts with sponges and towels, burning water off with gasoline, and renting helicopters to hover overhead with their giant rotors fanning the water off the court.

How a tournament staff faces the elements often dictates whether a tournament is merely postponed, or is canceled. An event in Australia had rain the day of its semifinals and tournament directors decided to abandon play for good. Another in South Orange, New Jersey, had rain for eight days during a seven-day tournament, but was able to finish on Monday, a day late, despite a deluge that stopped five minutes before the final and resumed five minutes afterward.

A tournament director must be a jack of all trades and a master of a half dozen. He must be familiar with tax law—sales tax, withholding tax for foreign players, and the tax status of the tournament itself. More than one foreign star has alluded to a mythical agent and begged the director not to withhold the required 30 percent of his prize money, threatening not to play again next year.

The director must understand insurance law and appreciate his potential liability for a wide range of accidents, from grandstand collapse to dented fenders in the parking lot. A director must have a sound knowledge of marketing: how to price tickets and how to sell the product. And without a grasp of advertising, the tournament could be stone-broke before the first ball is hit. Questions such as how much money should be spent on radio, TV, pamphlets and direct mail, posters, and public relations efforts have to be answered without flinching or fudging. The director should have equal quantities of huckster and Ringling Brothers in his blood in order to be able to schedule the most dramatic matches for center court. Even experienced officials at Wimbledon and Forest Hills have scheduled Chris Evert, Tracy Austin, or Ilie Nastase on outside courts and watched in horror as spectators trampled over hedges, fences, and each other to get closer to their heroes.

Many tournaments deal with some form of labor union. For example, the U.S. Open contracts with a ticket-sellers' and ticket-takers' union, a concessionaires' union, a parking-lot attendants' union, an electricians' union, a city employees' union, and two players' unions, to name a few. In order not to get featherbedded with overtime and superfluous workers, a familiarity with labor relations and contracts may be the difference between profit and disaster.

Finally, a tournament director should be a competent manager—of both people and business. Without proper handling of one, the other may go up in smoke. Since there is no one who is expert in every facet needed to stage a major circuit com-

Bjorn Borg, Mariana Simionescu, Arthur Ashe

The tour is a travel merry-go-round where even millionaires book coach air passage. Most players reach Wimbledon by limousine, though some walk from the tube station.

44

petition, most events have gigantic committees among which to divide up responsibilities. The U.S. Open, for instance, has over 500 staff members, volunteers, umpires, press liaisons, and USTA officials to ensure the Open functions efficiently.

The duties at indoor and outdoor events are not always interchangeable however. For example, when the U.S. Open changed sites from Forest Hills (clay) to Flushing Meadow (hard courts), there was no longer a need for a court maintenance crew. Not many grounds crews have the versatility to look after both grass and clay courts, although since England and Australia are the only two countries that stage major grass-court events, one wonders how long turf will continue to be a viable surface, considering its enormous maintenance costs. At least upkeep for clay courts has been mechanized. Tram lines are no longer laid down in chalk but are permanent fabric or lead tapes. Motorized rollers and brushers have reduced labor costs. Sophisticated cutting and rolling machines are used to manicure grass courts, but final trimming, weeding (weeds are called volunteers at Wimbledon), and chalking must be done by hand.

Sadly, the trend in America, France, and England is to construct all-weather maintenance-free courts, which have gained more acceptance by the switch of the U.S. Open to DecoTurf, a base of asphalt with a plastic coating on top. It requires no upkeep, but is hell on a player's feet.

Anyone still interested in producing a professional tennis tournament? If so, the unofficial handbook says that the five most critical factors are the *players, sponsor, site, television,* and *date.* The first two items present a Catch-22 situation. If you have the star players, securing a sponsor is easy. On the other hand, to get the players in the first place requires a sponsor. If you have both, television, whether commercial or public, is a certainty.

Dates are important because clever selection can mean you get better players for less prize money. For example, planning a tune-up tournament in the New York area the week before the U.S. Open is adroit scheduling. Many of the stars want to practice nearby the Flushing Meadow Stadium at similar court and lighting facilities. Furthermore, it probably helps recruiting if the event is not part of the official Grand Prix, with its bonus and ranking points. There is so much pressure during the year that a break from the regimen is a

John Lloyd

45

Despite disclaimers, all tennis has not moved to public parks.

Above: *The Queens Club, England*
Right: *The Lamar Hunt home, Dallas, Texas*
Opposite: *Monte Carlo, Monaco*

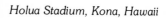

Holua Stadium, Kona, Hawaii

The Royal Albert Hall, London, England

longed-for oasis. Many players will sacrifice squeezing out the last sponsor dollar in order to practice under ideal conditions.

The venue is the easiest of all ingredients to determine. However, careful site selection can mean a difference of thousands of dollars. When looking for a location, the tournament director with savvy knows that there are four basic categories of courts: resort, public, club, and arena. Rent must be paid to the latter three, while the resort will often pay the tournament a fee for the right to be the host on the theory that the resulting publicity in newspapers and on television is worth more than static advertising.

How this approach works in practice is intriguing. The West Side Tennis Club, which for over fifty

48

years was the host of the U.S. Open and U.S. Nationals, received a rental over the past ten years of more than $125,000 a year. Certainly the club didn't need the publicity; West Side is a private club whose members were merely compensated for the use of their facilities. Caesar's Palace in Las Vegas, on the other hand, paid promoters $250,000 for the right to host the Jimmy Connors-John Newcombe "Heavyweight Challenge Match" televised by CBS. Caesar's Palace obviously felt that having its hotel identified on the scoreboard on TV for three hours, and occasionally mentioned by the TV announcers, was a better buy than 60-second commercial spots selling for $30,000 each. The range between what the West Side Tennis Club received and what Caesar's Palace paid was $375,000, which illustrates the incredible bargaining room available for an enterprising tournament director.

Television is a particularly treacherous mine field for a director to have to maneuver through. There are over 90 Grand Prix tournaments annually, only 15 percent of which are televised. But

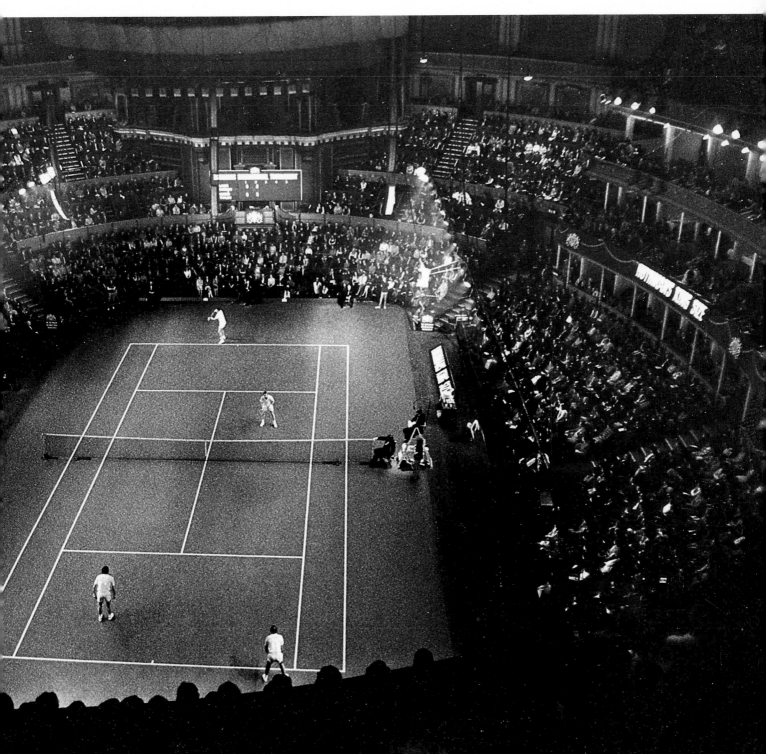

television is the bait that attracts every sponsor, and failure to secure a broadcast commitment has caused the withdrawal of dozens of sponsors. Although TV tennis is inexpensive to produce and assures advertisers an upgrade audience, the sport is not popular with affiliate stations which prefer boxing and football. Even when a tournament director can guarantee a top field and can sell half the advertising minutes to his sponsor, it is not inevitable that a network will buy the show. This uncertainty has led many tournament directors to band

are capable of providing sensational entertainment. All competent directors follow this advice, albeit tremulously, and attempt to sell 50 percent of their tickets before the field is even known. Most American summer-circuit tournaments sell between $75,000 to $150,000 in boxes before the first player takes the court.

This strategy was developed not on the basis of its marketing merits, but by necessity. After all, there are fewer than a dozen superstars and possibly another dozen who can sell tickets simply on the

Gstaad, Switzerland

together and create regular coverage through public broadcasting. Many of the successful camera techniques were developed for the extended PBS three- and four-hour telecasts.

There is a saying among tournament directors that the players should not be sold to the public, the event should be. This means that a director should never base his ticket sales on the prospect that one particular star will show up. The idea is that there are many excellent players in the world that

basis of their name—and it is physically impossible for them to play in all the important tournaments around the world.

Adroit player recruitment is essential if a tournament director is to be assured of a quality draw year after year. Some tournaments don't have to recruit at all. Because players know that their reputations are made at Wimbledon and the Open, they flock to these traditional events without coaxing. Other tournaments appeal to pros because of the

weather, the scenery, court conditions, hotel accommodations, prize money, access to other tournaments, and the dates on which they are played. All these factors influence a player differently from week to week, depending on whether he needs more practice or more rest, whether he needs more points or can't afford a bad loss which would drop his ATP standing and keep him out of main draws.

Ironically, the amount of prize money may not be the determining element to recruit a balanced field. The top 30 players are making so much money on the tour that the lure of a $250,000 purse is not compelling in itself. The ATP, which includes 200 of the top players but not one of the top 5, has perhaps oversold the game to sponsors in an effort to find more "job" opportunities for its constituents. Many tournament directors fear the power of the

Checking in and inspecting the draw is a ritual for every tournament player from junior to French champion.

Seedings offer predictions on how the scenario will resolve. Every player, except the number one, wants to prove the script wrong.

ATP to destroy or make an event by assigning certain players to one city rather than another.

Nonetheless, the tournament directors who endure are those who can look with equanimity at the multiple entanglements that must be sorted out for any tournament to succeed. A sense of perspective is as mandatory for a tournament director as is a deep second serve for a pro. Take the director at Forest Hills, for example, who 20 minutes before the start of his tournament was faced with a walkout by the concessionaires' union, a raging thunderstorm slated to begin as play started, and a warning of the summer's first power failure with half the matches scheduled for evening. If this curtain raiser didn't give a sense of perspective, then the bomb threat, followed by sniffing dogs and a helmeted bomb squad patrolling the stadium 10 minutes before the final did.

The table of a tournament director is a riotous feast. Some thrive on the variety, glamour, creativity, detail, and childish excitement of watching the production come alive. Others choke on it.

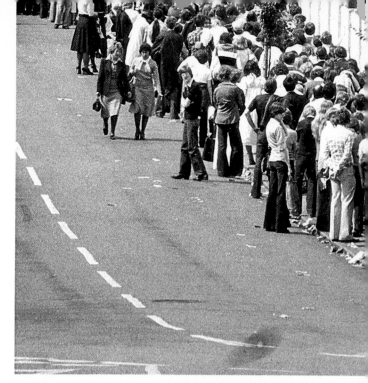

Fans at Wimbledon get so excited about their Championships that they will queue in tremendous lines and wait overnight in the rain to get seats or standing room for the finals.

Wendy Turnbull

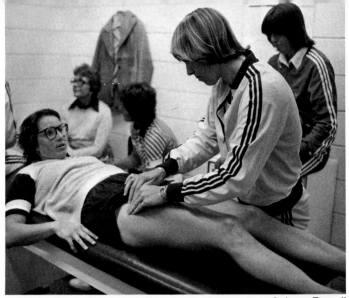

JoAnne Russell

The locker room is a miniature medical center whose function is to keep the athletes perpetually warmed up.

Zeljko Franulovic, Gene O'Connor, Jaime Fillol

If you can't reach the ball, you can't hit it.
Stretching is practiced as much as the
overhead.

Rain is a tournament director's nightmare. Solutions: a helicopter's rotors, a tarpaulin, a hot-air blower.

*Busman's holiday.
The women pros'
break on the tour is
often more sports.*

Rosie Casals, Wendy Turnbull

Yvona Brzkova, Maria Pinterova, Trish Faulkner, Jane Stratton, Regina Marsikova, Raquel Giscafre

Chris Evert

Mimmi Wikstedt, Lea Antonoplis

Renata Tomanova

Kym Ruddell, Barbara Jordan

Evonne Goolagong Cawley

Stacy Margolin   Barbara Potter   Mima Jausovec   Wendy Overton

Bettina Bunge   Dana Gilbert ▽   Regina Marsikova   Michele Gurdal ▽   Greer Stevens   Lesley Hunt ▽   Mona Guerrant   Sharon Walsh ▽

Ilana Kloss

Virginia Ruzici

Anne Smith

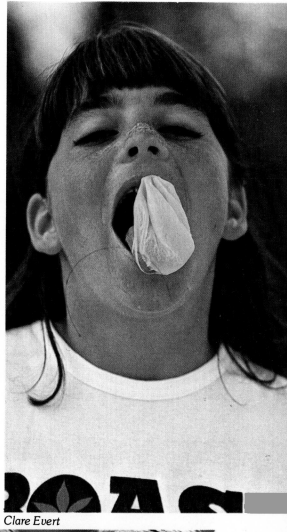

Clare Evert

Rosie Casals, Connie Spooner

Ann (Bunny) Bruning   Kate Latham

Helena Anliot

Sue Barker

Connie Spooner, Rosie Casals

68

Mary and Rod Laver

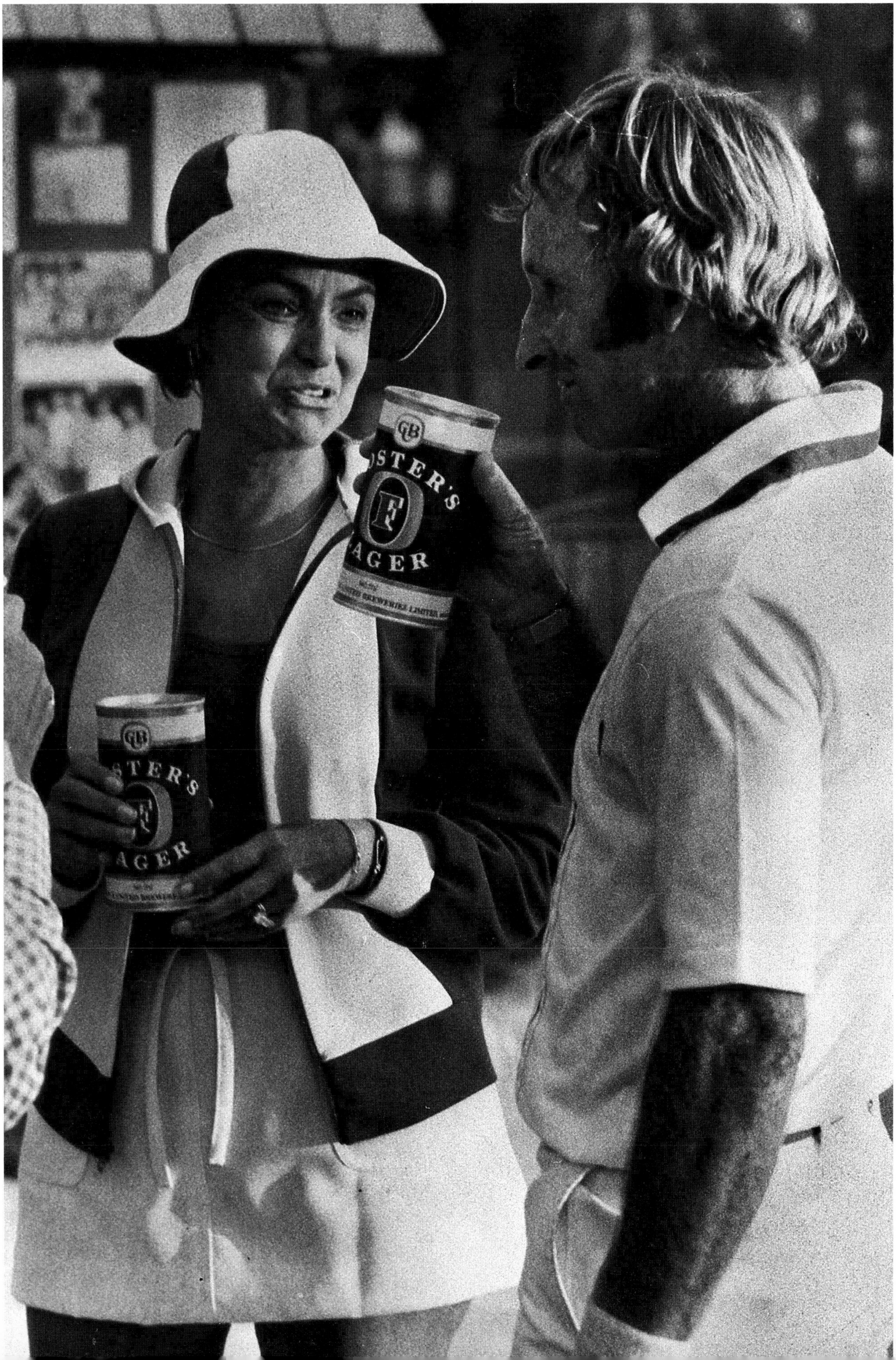

Tim Gullikson   Valerie Ziegenfuss ▽   Julie Anthony   Onny Parun ▽   Wojtec Fibak   Mareen (Peanut) Louie ▽

Ove Bengston   Wendy Turnbull ▽   Raul Ramirez   Leslie Allen ▽   Kym Ruddell   Guillermo Vilas ▽

Husbands and wives on the tour may share an identity as a couple that is totally apart from their on-court personalities.

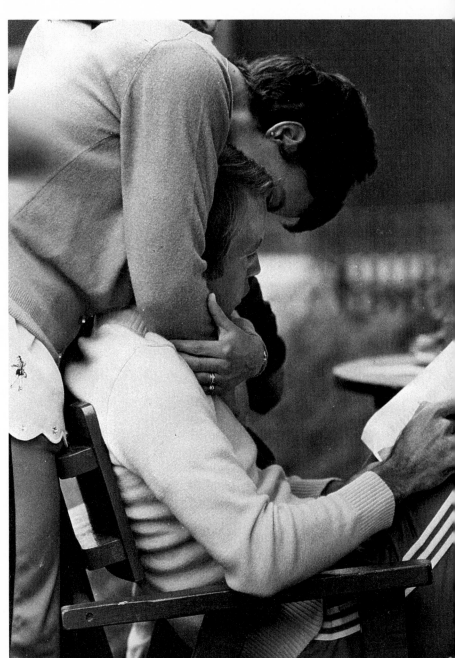

Kerry and Raz Reid

Dick and Sue Stockton

Stan and Margie Smith

Roger and Evonne Cawley

For many, the tour is a family affair.

Mrs. Russell and JoAnne

Mrs. Bunge and Bettina

Evonne Goolagong Cawley and Kelly

April Riessen and Jennifer

Barry Court and Danny

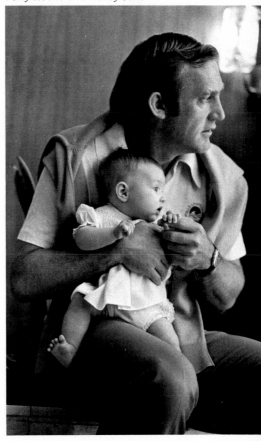

Tony Roche and Kelley Jane

Jean B. Chanfreau and Jean

The tournament is a potent mix of tradition, players, officials, prize money, press coverage, and galleries.

Mike Blanchard

Frank Hammond

Forest Hills press box

Wimbledon interview room

Ted Tinling

Bud Collins

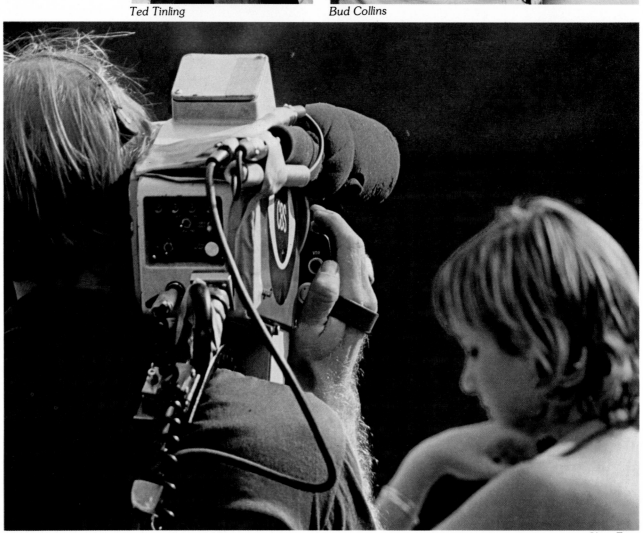

Chris Evert

All galleries come to watch their special favorites . . .

Renee Richards

84

. . . though some may be more partisan and fanatic than others.

Ilie Nastase

Ilie Nastase

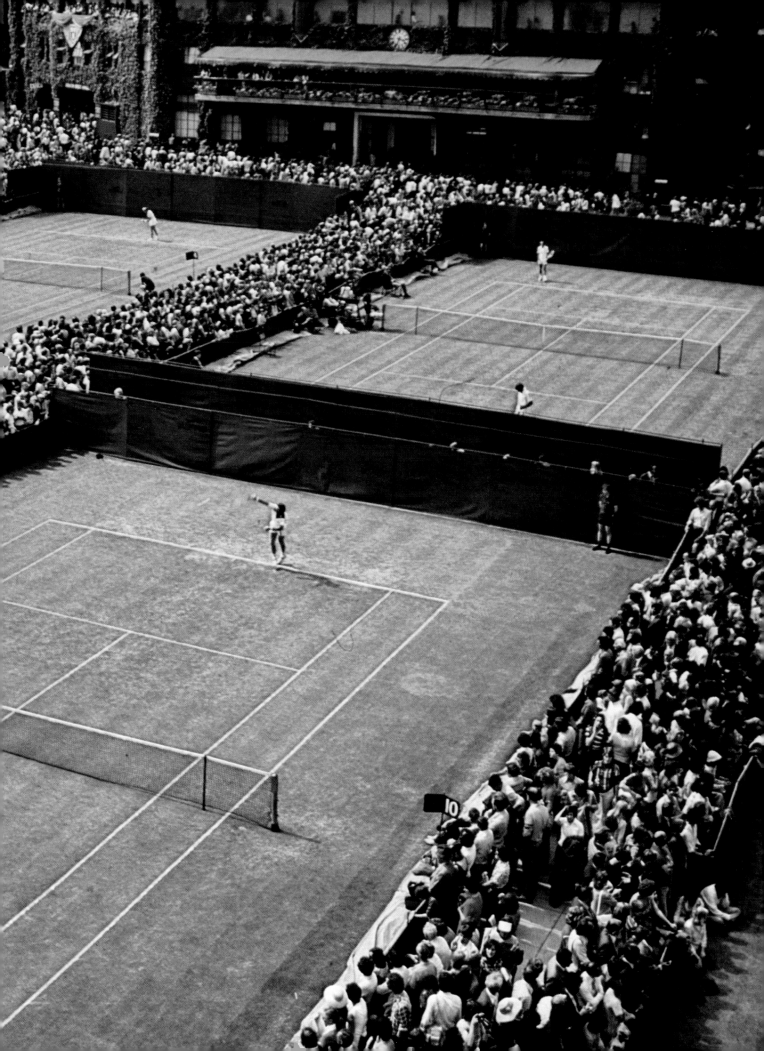

*Wimbledon and the U.S. Open are the
giant emblems on the sport's fabric,
with all other tennis merely trimming.*

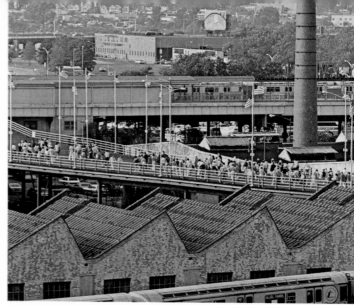

The new U.S. Open site at Flushing Meadow, New York, cost more than $9 million to complete and is the first major tennis facility to be built in America in over fifty years.

Chris Evert

Chris Evert

3

The Superpros

Chris Evert may be the most celebrated athlete in sports history. Early in her career communications technology focused the attention of television audiences all over the globe on this dynamic young woman who was taking control of women's tennis. When Chris was 16, she appeared on the cover of *Newsweek*, propelling her fame and her name into still larger arenas. It may be impossible for any player to equal the accumulated acclaim lavished on Chrissie in the 1970s.

The initial uproar over Evert arose at Forest Hills in 1973 when, barely 16 years old, she reached the semifinals. The unique story line wasn't that this young unranked player did so well in the U.S. Open—it was how she did it. Three times in her opening-round matches, Chris was down match point to foes who were supposed to blow her away. Chris came back often and with great daring. And she was graceful and pretty. Remove the youthful dew or the ponytail, and Chris's Cinderella story might have made very sleepy copy. But men wanted to protect her from the wicked world, women wanted to mother her, and teenagers wanted to marry her. And everyone wanted her to thrash the daylights out of her opponents. Chris Evert had unusual appeal long before she became world champion.

She is adored everywhere but at Wimbledon, where spectators want their heroes to be demonstrative about their feelings—like Billie Jean King or Virginia Wade. The British confuse Evert's icy nerve with a lack of flesh and blood. It's a bad rap. She is warm, sensitive, and perceptive. And her romances with Jimmy Connors and Burt Reynolds and her marriage to John Lloyd should have proven to English galleries that this woman is not just cold coals on a hearthstone.

In July 1973 Evert began one of the most famous records in sports. Until she was beaten by Tracy Austin in 1979, she had won 125 straight matches on clay. It is doubtful if ever again a tennis player will remain unbeaten for so long. The miracle of her game is that it is fashioned not with a giant serve, booming forehand, or killer volley, but with a force field of hypnotizing concentration. No one rattles Chris Evert. Few beat her either.

Vitas Gerulaitis is known affectionately as the Disco Kid. The sobriquet fits. He is as fast with his feet as with his hands. A resident member of Studio 54 and Regine's, the world's most electric discoteques, Gerulaitis is tennis's most electric athlete: his celebrity status off court is matched by his dynamism on court. He is a veritable streak at the net, where his giant hands move his racket in the blink of his eyes.

If Vitas has a weakness, it is his second serve, which occasionally deteriorates into a wobbly arc over the net. But foes attack this frailty at their peril, so alert is Vitas to the counterpunch. Some also have said that he is strung out on the disco scene, but what few realize is that Vitas has a strong sense of family and lives in the compound he has created for his parents and sister Ruta, who is fast rising in the women's ranks.

Vitas' wild blond hair looks like leftovers from an angel's cut, giving him the appearance as he dashes across the court of a truant choirboy late for a solo. In keeping with his breakaway speed, Gerulaitis has a passion for fast cars; his Porsche Turbo, two Rolls Royces, and a Lamborghini share garage space with two dozen rackets and size-11 tennis shoes. But don't be fooled by the tinsel trappings. This man practices harder than he dances and is serious enough about the game to have developed a youth foundation offering free tennis clinics to inner-city players in New York.

Gerulaitis has amassed more important titles before age 25 than most stars see in a lifetime. He won the Italian Championships in 1977 against partisan officials, slow clay, and the entire Italian Davis Cup team. He dominated Dallas indoors (1978), the crown jewel of the WCT galaxy, and captured the Australian Open (1978) on grass, proving that he excels on any surface. Later in 1978 he showed he's a money winner by zapping the field at the Forest Hills Invitational and devouring $100,000 in the process. Vitas has his own line of cologne, rackets, and sweaters. One day he will be a dance. Vitas with me, anyone?

Jimmy Connors does things alone. Since its inception in 1974, he has not joined the ATP (the players' union). But he once sued the ATP and its officers for keeping him out of the French Open. Yet despite nagging litigation and other aggravations, the hostile ATP computer has ranked Connors number one in the world since it first spat out data five years ago.

Connors' five-year domination of the game has verged on monopoly. He won two of the quickest finals in Wimbledon and U.S. Open history in 1974. He won the Open again in 1976 and 1978. But more interestingly, he always reaches the finals. The man simply doesn't have bad losses or bad days.

Although only 5'10" and 155 pounds, his physical and psychological strengths are herculean. In the middle of his lawsuit against the players in 1974, he went onto center court for the Wimbledon finals against Ken Rosewall, one of the most popular pros of all time and an overwhelming sentimental favorite for the title he had never won. The locker room before the match was icy with tension. No one spoke to Connors; outside, the British gallery was all in Rosewall's corner. Connors bore that antagonism and turned Rosewall upside down in 55 minutes, 6–1, 6–1, 6–4.

His consistency is virtually unrivaled. So excellent is his performance that at the beginning of 1979 his point average would have dropped 20 points if he *won* a $100,000 tournament. He had to win a $125,000 event to maintain his average.

Much has been made of Connors' symbiotic relationship with his mother. Psychiatrists may differ about the powerful influence Gloria exerts over her son. Perhaps too much attention has been focused on the sinews that bind them, although with the revelation that Jimmy had been secretly married to a *Playboy* model early in 1979, perhaps some of the speculation will abate. One thing is certain: On court Jimmy Connors is utterly his own man. Sometimes to his detriment. In his nonstop attack on both the ball and his opponents, he refuses to compromise and play the safe shot. There are no subtle approaches or angles to unnerve a foe. He goes for broke all the time, and on rare occasions winds up broke, refusing to temper his aggression.

His heresies of flashing a middle finger at the crowd, dropping his sweat pants to moon a handful of spectators at the U.S. Open, or refusing to play on the Davis Cup team have offended many. But it is tricky to tamper with the chemistry of a champion. Change one element of his temperament and you may lose the essential athlete who has done so much to revolutionize tennis. No one before or since has ever hit the ball so hard for so long in a single tennis match—or tennis career—as James Scott Connors.

More people had heard of **Tracy Austin** by the time she was 14 than heard of three-time Wimbledon champion Maureen Connolly during her lifetime. This is because the flame of the modern superstar is fed crazily by current communications technology. Tracy was barely a teenager when she appeared on the cover of *Sports Illustrated* (with its 12.7 million readership) as the most amazing player of her age in tennis history. At 14 she had reached the quarterfinals of the U.S. Open and by the end of the year had become the youngest player ever to be ranked among the world's top 10. She appeared on the covers of all the major tennis magazines and was named rookie of the year two years before she could legally drive. In 1978 she reached the semifinals of the U.S. Open and promptly turned pro. Before her sixteenth birthday she had won two major fall tournaments and was ranked fifth in the world.

Tracy Austin is not a dimpled teenager with nothing but blank stares for conversation. She is a gritty lady who had to learn early to parry with a press asking provoking questions. Her responses are as brisk and straightforward as her backswing.

Austin's age and accomplishments make her career different from that of Chris Evert, whose domination of the women's ranks came early, but nothing nearly so soon as this ingenue. Austin's strokes are a mirror of Evert's game: two-handed backhand, incredible concentration, and the consistency of a metronome. Indeed, Tracy may become better than Evert. The Californian has a better build for the game, slender and sleek, which should help her develop a punishing serve and volley. Just imagine a teenager with the steadiness of a surgeon and the cutting power of a buzz saw. Wait till Tracy Austin grows up.

Pam Shriver is an extroverted teenager with an

extroverted tennis game. She is the tallest woman in the top 10 and serves and volleys like "Jackie" in the Bean Stalk. Her personality is as refreshing as her strokes. She has the capacity to smile at herself and things around her. But don't be fooled by Shriver's sunny disposition. Her temperament is that rare blend of calm and courage.

In the 1978 U.S. Open, Shriver beat the world's number-one player, Martina Navratilova, in the semifinal and then battled Chris Evert tooth for tooth before the defending champion's experience squeezed out a victory. And Shriver wasn't awed by the moment—a world-record 20,000 stadium fans and another 20 million watching on television.

Pam is the first superstar to use the oversize Prince racket, and the fact that she is supersize herself makes the prospects of passing her gloomy indeed. Many of tennis's tall women before her—Christine Truman, Betty Stove, and Karen Krantzke—had good serves and ample power, but little range and no flexibility to alter a game plan gone astray. Shriver has the latent machinery to smother an opponent from anywhere on the court. So great is her aptitude for learning new shots that an opponent probing for a weakness risks Shriver's turning the deficiency into a strength.

Jimmy Connors once sneered at a reporter, "I sure wouldn't relish the prospect of playing someone like me." Shriver has the talent to say the same thing, but the charm to let you know she's simply telling the truth.

John McEnroe leads the wave of youths marauding the tennis circuit. At 18 he became the youngest man in history to reach the Wimbledon semifinals, doing so after toiling through the qualifying rounds—also a first. It was no fluke. Two months later, after he won the Intercollegiate championship for Stanford as a freshman, he was ranked fifteenth in the world. In 1978 he attained superstar status, first reaching the semifinals of the U.S. Open and then taking Hartford, San Francisco, London, and Stockholm, where he crunched Bjorn Borg, 6–3, 6–4. In just seven weeks he won $120,000 in singles and doubles competition. He rocketed to fourth in the world, and in the quinella standings, the locker-room statistics that unofficially rate players according to their combined singles and doubles records, McEnroe stood as the unequivocal number one.

Doubles is a useful tool for measuring the overall skill of a player, and it is particularly telling if a young pro shows an instinct for the tandem game. It demonstrates a sure knowledge of court distances and angles and a special aptitude for volleying, the most difficult stroke in tennis to master. To understand the most complex ingredients of the sport so early in one's career is a certain sign of genius.

Most tennis prodigies spend so much time practicing that they risk burning out before their talent matures. McEnroe, though, didn't spend every moment of his childhood playing tennis. He was a gifted high school soccer and basketball player who spent his summers concentrating on tennis. The fact that he developed so proficiently as a junior, without having played an extraordinary amount of tennis, is further evidence that he is unique.

As meteoric as McEnroe's rise has been, however, there are still dramatic progressions he will make. Mighty Mac will lose periodically on clay until he has a deeper understanding of the subtleties of that surface. Yet, he did defeat Guillermo Vilas, one of the world's top clay courters, in the 1979 Pepsi Grand Slam third-place playoff to prove that his time may come sooner, not later. But his major mark should first be established on grass, at Wimbledon, where Bjorn Borg and Jimmy Connors both give up the net and play in the backcourt. Against lesser men, Borg and Connors can make this grand gesture. But so devastating are his lefty serve and volley that McEnroe will make them choke on their lack of aggression on turf.

As much has been written about John's fiery temper as about his forehand. He should know better: he's no punk; he's had advantages. But douse the fire in John's blood and you may cool the rocket in his swinging serve. The dilemma is joined. Solve it and McEnroe will blaze a career in tennis that will terrorize all pursuers. Don't, and he'll terrorize opponents *and* officials forever.

Martina Navratilova has more natural ability than any woman who has ever played tennis. Blessed with broad shoulders and powerful legs, she can physically dominate an opponent as no one ever could. Being a left-hander makes Martina an even more imposing foe. Her southpaw serve sweeps opponents clear off the court, and if the spin can be returned at all it is usually a harmless sitter fit to be killed instantly.

Her head was once her Achilles' heel. She sometimes played without any understanding of the extraordinary skills she had at the tip of her racket, not knowing that it was occasionally necessary to temper brute strength with guile.

Martina first crashed through her psychological sound barrier by winning the 1978 Virginia Slims circuit. She proved her performance was not simply luck by destroying arch-rival Chris Evert at Wimbledon three months later. With these twin jewels in her crown, Martina was recognized (finally) as the world's number one, a distinction experts had predicted for her far earlier. Ms. Evert, however, didn't relish the prospect of someone else wearing the women's crown, no matter how briefly, so she plunged herself into a competitive training regimen that nudged Navratilova back down to number two. Then Navratilova promptly won the 1979 Avon Championships, propelling her back to number one. This rivalry, sure to be tagged "two for the seesaw," will undoubtedly continue as Martina interfaces her new confidence with her old forehand.

Navratilova supplies needed drama for the tour's script writers. She defected from Czechoslovakia at 18 and sought asylum in the United States. Within six months she was ranked among the top five players in the world. Martina has the unique kind of personality that allows her to giggle demurely, eat her favorite flavor of ice cream, and disco the night away, and the next afternoon to turn around and ram a ball down her opponent's throat. Chris Evert and the rest of the gang had best not keep their eyes far from the hand that eats the ice cream.

At age 15 **Bjorn Borg** played his first Davis Cup match for Sweden, winning it against New Zealand star Onny Parun. At 17 he won the French Championships, considered by the pros to be the most grueling test of skill and endurance on the tour. The following year he won the Italian Open and then his second French Championships.

Considered by experts to have been the most advanced teenager in tennis annals, Borg's strengths have matured. He seems to have escaped the fate of the last great whiz kid, Lew Hoad, who 20 years ago fizzled out physically after twice winning at Wimbledon. The svelte Swede has already won Wimbledon three consecutive years, a record unequaled since Englishman Fred Perry performed the triple feat 40 years ago. But Borg hasn't just established statistical marks in the game, he has engineered a style of play that a world of teenagers is imitating. With an exaggerated western forehand grip, he smacks the ball with all his might. His powerful swing produces a wild top spin that befuddles opponents who are caught in the dilemma of trying to chase the spinning parabola or intercept the dipping ball before it bounces.

Borg was the first "pop" star in tennis, requiring police escorts from the Wimbledon dressing room to the court in order to shield him from bands of British school girls who fainted at the sight of him. His dramatic hitting style has made opponents swoon too. Borg has won on all surfaces and in hostile surroundings, and for three months in the summer of 1978 it appeared as if he might never lose another match. First he won the Italian Championships, which smart players won't enter because of partisan officials who call line balls out without flinching and fans who toss hot coins at foes who torment their Roman Davis Cup idols. Then he won the French Open, followed by three Davis Cup matches, and finally Wimbledon.

Borg is one of several superstars who travels with a coach/manager—Leonart Bergelin. His coach is not a crutch, but instead, a presence. He is Borg's friend, a companion who is loyal only to his needs and hurts and who can prevent the pain from carrying over into the next match. Borg doesn't forget his loyalty to Bergelin or to anyone—an unusual trait in tennis.

Physically, Borg attacks the ball so ruthlessly that he may one day be a casualty of his own force. Perhaps the sinew that whips his forehand and backhand with such searing velocity will suddenly snap. But not before center courts and record books are littered with his victims.

Guillermo Vilas is a protean man. Aside from being the world's number-one tennis player in 1977, he is a published poet, an expert on the disparate sounds of modern music, and a sportsman nonpareil who would sooner insult a lady than accept an unfair line call.

Vilas's standards of physical fitness are punishing but profitable. He has set records for simultaneous endurance and high performance that a formula-one racing engine would envy. In 1977 he won 11 straight Grand Prix tournaments, including 5 in the dead of America's hottest summer. Four weeks in a row he played finals on Monday nights and then scurried on to the next event, a round or sometimes two behind the rest of the field—a format deemed so inhuman that it was abandoned by the game's governors the following season. He simply never lost. Vilas's streak lasted 80 straight singles matches, a feat that may never be equaled. (That year he coasted home—the $300,000 Grand Prix bonus winner.)

The muscular Argentine has won on every playing surface—the South African Open on ce- ment in 1977, the U.S. Open on clay in 1977, and the Australian Open on grass in 1979. Only the sport's selected few have the versatility to adapt to such a variety of conditions. Vilas demonstrates a flexibility that is fashioned from an eclectic blend of mental and muscle power. He doesn't destroy foes with the strength of his stroke alone. Anyone who has ever been on court with Vilas is aware of the massive energy he propels into his matches.

Some point to Vilas's Draconian relationship with Ion Tiriac, who acts as his coach and business agent, as the chink in this gladiator's armor. Don't believe it. Tiriac is Vilas's mantra, his focal point in times of crisis and glory. Few people in sports have set their sights on single targets and then accomplished their goals with such clarity and dignity as Vilas.

McEnroe may be the most versatile all-around athlete in tennis that the United States has ever produced.

Vitas has a reputation for fast—fast money, fast women, and fast lines.

Gerulaitis is exceptionally close to his family.

Ruta Gerulaitis

Vitas Gerulaitis, Sr., Ruta Gerulaitis, Donna Gerulaitis

The Gerulaitis Youth Clinics in New York City offer free tennis lessons to inner-city kids.

A modern American heroine.

The two most important men in Evert's life are her husband, John Lloyd, and her father, Jim Evert.

The flip side of Chris.

117

Concentration is Evert's best stroke.

*A folk hero around the world—
particularly among women.*

In motion and repose—immutable.

Fiancée Mariana Simionescu

In partial bloom, already a superstar.

127

Austin's backhand and concentration equal Evert's.

At Wimbledon Austin received what one expects to be the first of many trophies.

Connors can relax as well and as hard as he can play.

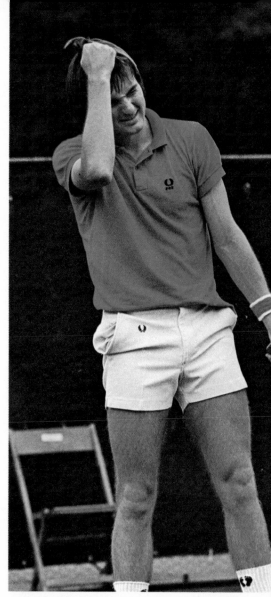

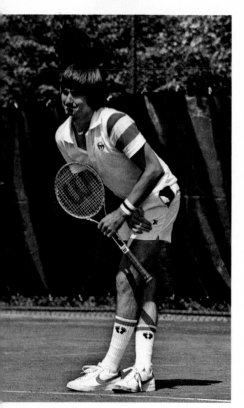

Ilie Nastase

Harry Hopman, Vitas Gerulaitis, Sr.

Because of his small size (5'10", 155 pounds), Connors must use 100 percent of his energy on every shot in order to generate his awesome power.

Martina Navratilova has the power and raw athletic ability to dominate women's tennis for 10 years.

Chris Evert

140

Few people in sports have set their sights on single targets and accomplished their goals with such clarity and dignity as Vilas.

Ali McGraw

Ion Tiriac

146

*Shriver is an extroverted teenager with
an extroverted tennis game.*

Ilie Nastase

4

The Passion

Whether a player smacks his serve like a Wimbledon winner or a baffled beginner, the pleasure or pain he senses is an individual experience. But during a tennis match, expressions of emotion may be the only clues to a player's strategy, the breaks of the game, or just how the player is feeling that day. Although some players have the inscrutable control of Chris Evert, some, like John McEnroe and Ilie Nastase, permit their feelings to run berserk.

To illustrate the sweep of passions that punctuate the game, the expressive sides of top professionals are shown here. That is not to say that only they can feel strongly about their game, but professional tennis is the ultimate experience, and if John McEnroe misses a volley at set point at Wimbledon, his understanding of how difficult that volley was is a measure of the anger he feels. The hacker flubbing a floater in Central Park may explode in fury, but his miss hardly has the proportions of McEnroe's.

The professionals know there is no sure shot in tennis. Chris Evert and Guillermo Vilas have missed short overheads perched teasingly next to the net, although not often. But often enough so they understand the difficulty of their craft, which is why they suffer and rejoice more intensely after errors or triumphs than the rest of us.

There is a chestnut as old as the game itself that consoles, "The breaks even out." Don't believe it. The flukes of the game rarely are dispatched even-steven, and they come in many forms: bad bounces, ricochets off the racket, sun glaring in the eyes, mischievous winds, and of course the infamous net cord. How a player responds to these quirks is reflected in the twists of his body, the contortions of his face—and often only a photographer with the quick eyes and trigger finger of a sheriff can capture these shifting passions.

Rarely is there a pattern to emotional displays in tennis. Anger, intensity, despair, weariness, resignation, and triumph are all part of a player's day. Although one won't witness sweat and grimace at the beginning of a semifinal, fatigue and frustration wear on an athlete progressively as the match winds to its close. Anger often appears without warning, long after the real reason for the aggravation has passed. For example, an opponent's stalling tactics may be tolerated for a set or more, but after he questions a close call in the final set, the heretofore patient player's hostility may be unleashed like the whistle of a pressure cooker. But for the player angry with himself, release is hard to come by.

The strain and intensity of the number-one seed is light-years apart from the anxiety of a qualifier who has squeaked through three preliminary rounds just to make it into the main draw. The player who is expected to win the tournament is playing to keep from losing, to continue to merit his lofty rank. The qualifier is hustling to show that he is worthy. His appetites and emotions are near term—the qualifier can't expect to last too long. But if there is a common ground for the two, it is their pursuit of a single conquest. There is nothing that shouts louder than the professional's tragic credo, "You are only as good as your last triumph."

Every pro deals with his frenzy differently. The pressure is monstrous. It surfaces in moments of pain, despair, and celebration. It is often stifled—a stiff upper lip, seeming ambivalence, the quiet control of a Zen master, are all disguises. Indeed, one player's mania may turn court gestures into court jesters.

Wojtec Fibak

The Passions:
Anger

Virginia Wade

Mark Edmonson

Anand Amritraj

Tom Okker

Frustration

John McEnroe

Roscoe Tanner

John Newcombe

Lesley Hunt

Ken Rosewall

160

Pam Shriver

Olga Morozova

Martina Navratilova

Andrew Patterson

Despair

Kim Warwick

Betty Stove

Tracy Austin

Exhaustion

Bob Lutz

Evonne Goolagong Cawley

Harold Solomon

Billie Jean King

Triumph

Tom Gorman

168

Anne Hobbs, Sue Mappin, Michele Tyler, Sue Barker, Virginia Wade

David Lloyd, Mark Cox, and team

Roger Taylor, Sue Barker

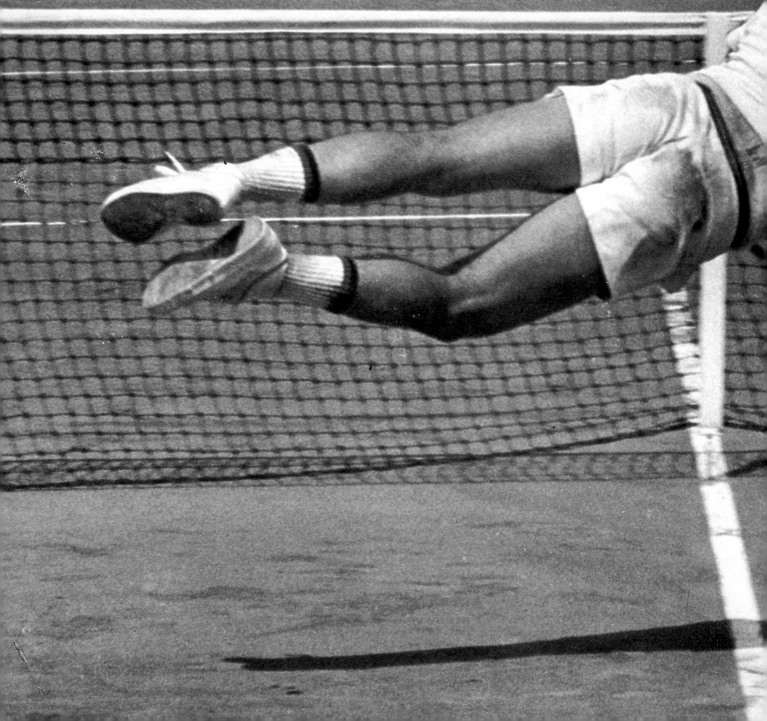

5

Eric Deblicker

The Play

Beth Norton

Sharon Walsh

Margaret Court

Sherwood Stewart, Fred McNair

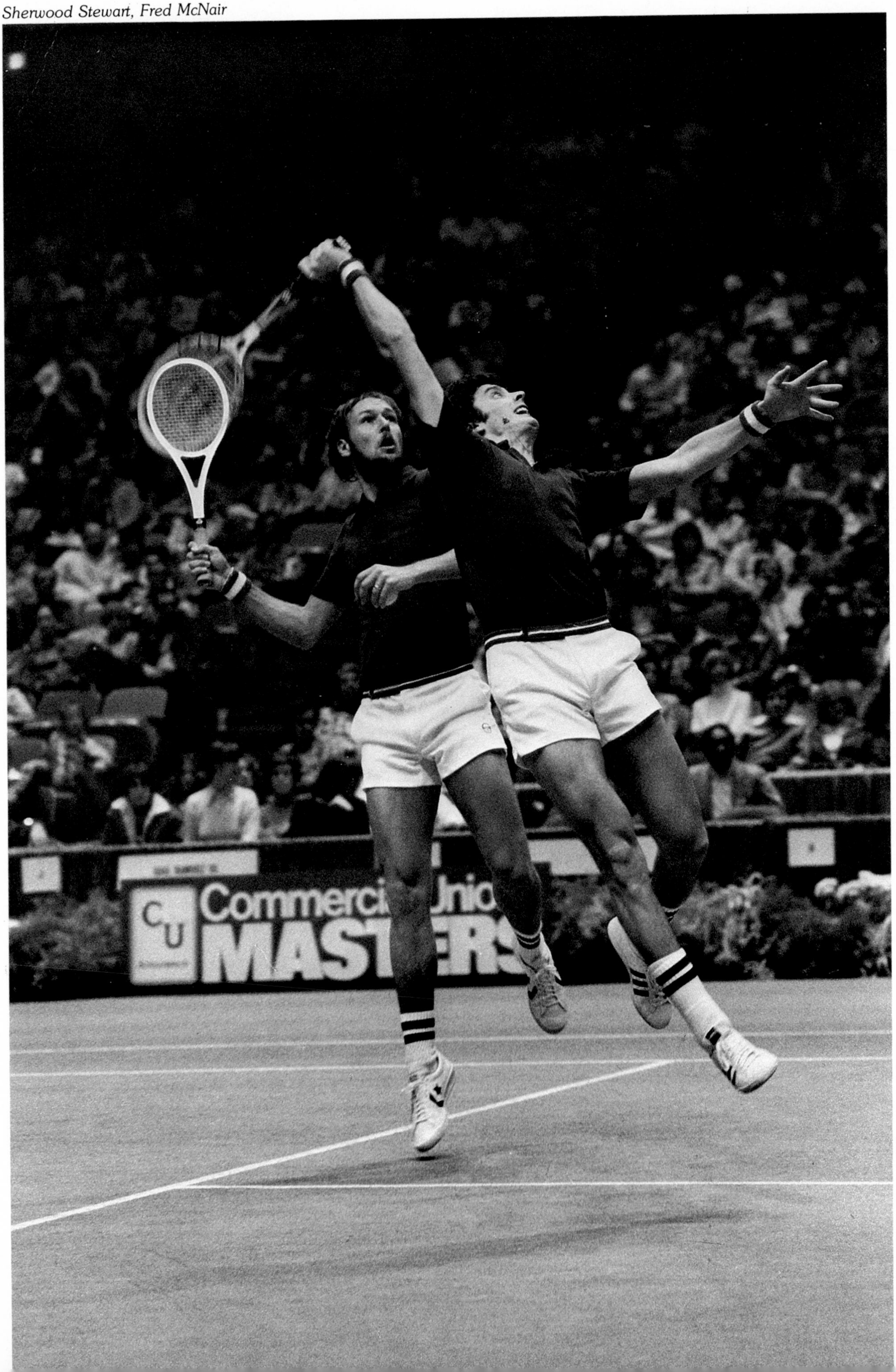

Brian Gottfried

Peter Fleming

Ilie Nastase, Jimmy Connors

Jimmy Connors

Ilie Nastase

182

Vitas Gerulaitis

Dianne Fromholtz

Sherwood Stewart

184

Evonne Goolagong Cawley

Hana Mandlikova

Wendy Turnbull

Virginia Wade

Dick Stockton, Donna Stockton

Julie Heldman

Greer Stevens

188

Marita Redondo

Francoise Dürr

Rosie Casals

Rod Laver

Barbara Jordan

T. E. Gullikson

Harold Solomon

Adriano Panatta

194

Peanut Louie

Jimmy Connors

Billie Jean King

John Newcombe

Manuel Orantes

Arthur Ashe

Tom Okker

Olga Morozova

Roscoe Tanner

Dick Stockton

Betsy Nagelsen

Bjorn Borg

Gene Mayer

Adriano Panatta

Eddie
Dibbs

Mary Carillo

Kathy Jordan

Kerry Reid

207

. . . left-handed

Maria Pinterova . . . right-handed

Roscoe Tanner

Pam Teeguarden

Ann Kiyomura

Jeanne Evert

Jimmy Connors

Ray Moore

Chris Evert

Jimmy Connors

Martina Navratilova

6

Ken Rosewall

The Twilighters

Every sport has an age when its heroes perform at the highest level. "Reaching your peak" is a critical phase in an athlete's career—when physical and mental skills blend in ringing unison. The fabled Bill Tilden didn't win a National Championship until he was 29, and Wimbledon and U.S. Open champion Vic Seixas didn't compete overseas until he was 28. Bjorn Borg, on the other hand, had won three Wimbledon and three French Open titles by the age of 22. Clearly the peaks of professional tennis careers are being reached at steadily younger ages, as teaching techniques progress so rapidly that 12-year-olds can now hit top-spin backhand lobs, shots that Manolo Santana and Rod Laver invented only 20 years ago.

Players like Lew Hoad and Chuck McKinley burned brightly quickly, then were gone by the time they were 25. Others, like Ken Rosewall and Pancho Gonzalez, spanned three decades of play. At 42, Rosewall beat Eddie Dibbs, 26, the winner of the 1978 Grand Prix, and Ilie Nastase, 29, the reigning Masters champion. Gonzalez, 41, beat Laver when the redhead was still ranked among the top four players in the world. Other mere mortals try to sort out their peaks and valleys, prolonging one, postponing the other, but in truth they are only different sides of the same equation.

John Newcombe, Arthur Ashe, Billie Jean King, Evonne Goolagong, Virginia Wade, Rod Laver, Roy Emerson, Tony Roche, Margaret Court, and Ken Rosewall are all past their competitive peaks. Yet a half-dozen times a year their skills emerge intact, like a campfire that suddenly bursts into its brightest light and then recedes to a warm glow.

What happens to the chemistry of a superstar in twilight? Although the "peak" represents the consummate genius, an aging athlete is not betrayed simply by failing strength and speed. Simultaneously, confidence can be undercut by a deadly stroke that renders useless all the precious knowledge garnered from a lifetime of experience and success. But the most destructive element to a player's performance is the expansion of his outside interests. Whether it is a growing family or a proliferation of business interests, the broadening process reduces the intensity of focus on tennis itself. Newcombe, Ashe, Laver, and King are walking conglomerates with far-ranging endorsements and investments. Their playing records have dimmed in direct proportion to the demands of their off-court enterprises.

Periodically all twilighters make valiant efforts to reharness their energies, reduce distractions, and return to the competitive mainstream. This is known as the "comeback." Pancho Gonzalez retired and came back four times, Billie Jean King twice, John Newcombe and Arthur Ashe once each. Competitive bile does not cool easily; it bubbles beneath the surface long after peak performance is plausible.

But within the galaxy of twilighters, there is now a phenomenon that has added a new universe for the veteran superstars—the Living Legends of Tennis. This special group of superstars 35 years or older includes Laver, Rosewall, Newcombe, Ashe, Marty Riessen, Cliff Drysdale, Emerson, Fred Stolle, Roche, and Santana, a field that most Grand Prix operators would be thrilled to assemble. Theirs is a world still close to the rocketry of Borg and Connors. No middle-aged paunch there. In fact, as a group they may be the finest assembly of athletes for their age anywhere. As proof, each one of these twilighters plays the tour from time to time, kicking up chaos with the computer ranking system that can't crank into its criteria the uneven but penetrating performance of an aging idol.

It isn't easy to get old. Harder for athletes because their careers fade when most workers are entering the primes of their lives. The sad sagas of old ballplayers hanging on when their bodies cannot perform are legion; the physical and fiscal disintegration of a tired athlete is not pretty. So, it is no accident that players like Ashe, Newcombe, Stolle, and Laver never have to volley a ball again to survive financially. Yet they continue to discipline their heads and hearts for the severity of the tour simply to meet its challenge.

Tennis's twilighters accomplish a rare excellence. Each faces the prospect of diminishing skills with an eclectic blend of realism and courage.

Roy Emerson

Fred Stolle

Cliff Richey

Cliff Drysdale

Marty Riessen

Arthur Ashe

Margaret Court

Ken Rosewall, Rod Laver

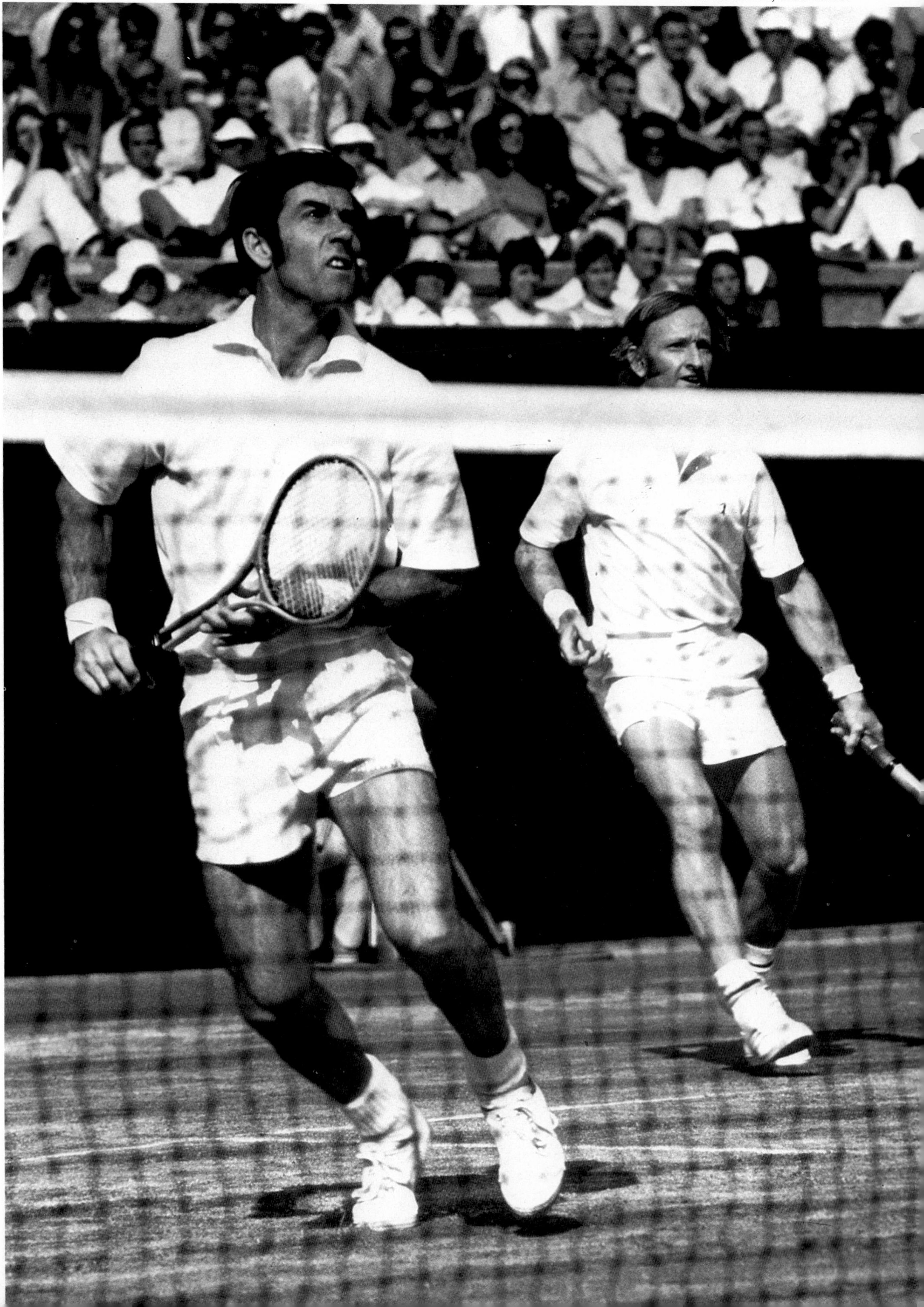

Frew McMillan, Bob Hewitt

Stan Smith, Bob Lutz

Billie Jean King

Martina Navratilova

Ken Rosewall

John Newcombe

237

René Lacoste   Henri Cochet

7

Jacques Brugnon

René Lacoste
Henri Cochet
Jean Borotra

Jean Borotra

Not the End

If ever there was a perfect target for a mother's exhortation, "You just don't know when to stop," it should be reserved for the Grand Masters, an exclusive corps of yesterday's tennis heroes who are at least 45 years old. They travel around the United States, and to Wimbledon, as an elite band of eight men who are perhaps the finest athletes for their age in the world. The names of Pancho Gonzalez, Frank Sedgman, Vic Seixas, Torben Ulrich, Pancho Segura, Neale Fraser, Ham Richardson, Frankie Parker, and Lew Hoad are inscribed in the sport's record books for winning a blaze of Wimbledons, U.S. Nationals, and Davis Cups. But what matters to these men now isn't their past records, it is their current ability to perform against their peers. What may have been lost in speed has been preserved in style. The tempo has been rearranged to a gentler rhythm, but the stroke pattern is timeless—undoubtedly a better learning tool for most of us than the crashing pace of Connors or Borg.

There is as much money in the Grand Masters today as for the first Open events. Fifteen thousand dollars split eight ways is as much as Wimbledon offered until a few years ago. And remember, this is supplemental income, which is incentive enough for the Grand Masters to keep in remarkable condition. Rather than letting their skills revert to memories in instruction books and old clippings, they continue instead as a living art form for the rest of the retired world to imitate. Indeed, they may never stop.

Medical opinion varies on the issue of when the rest of us should stop: instructions range from "No singles after 50" to a more Olympian direction, "Play forever." There will be more than thirty million Americans over age 65 by 1980, and some will play only doubles, just as the doctor has ordered. Others will continue to play singles as long as jogging messiahs like Dr. George Sheehan preach their exercise magic.

Dr. Sheehan, 61, was an intercollegiate runner who gave it up for tennis during his internship as a cardiologist. Then, in his mid-40s, he returned to running after he broke his hand playing tennis. Sheehan has become famous for his advice to elderly office-bound types who wonder if they are too old to start (or continue) jogging. "Your body knows best. Listen to your body for signs of pain or strain." Until then, he contends, we can jog or play tennis at will. Clearly there are growing numbers of enthusiasts who are doing their utmost to prove that the motto of the United States Tennis Association— "Our game . . . for a lifetime"—is valid.

Certainly there is more to a senior's passion for the game than copying the form of the great players or the dream of living forever—not everyone over 55 plays tennis because it is healthy, although it is. Tennis has a narcotic effect on its participants. Once snared by the lure of the game, the player is usually hooked for life.

The element of hand-to-hand combat in tennis is not part of sports like golf, where players compete against the course rather than each other. But in tennis, 50 percent of the people who step on the court lose. This dreary statistic grates on some athletes and goads them to neutralize the odds by striving to improve. Others are content to be locked in the struggle—win or lose. The latter pertains especially to the veterans. Why else would an aging executive with arthritis in both hips cruise to the neighborhood bubble every Saturday and wince with every forehand? The compulsion of seniors to trot onto center court, despite failing strength and eyesight, awkward strokes, and pain in their limbs, is testimony to the stubbornness of the human will.

There are formal singles competitions for older players, ranging from ages 35 to 45 (mere infants in the group) to the more patriarchal divisions—55s, 65s, 70s, 75s, and 80s. Indeed, U.S. National Singles Championships exist in each of these categories, and if a lightning serve has become an arching moon ball, competitive resolve has not dimmed whatsoever.

And, there is even a national association of players over 65—the Super Seniors—whose headquarters in Charlottesville, Virginia, is the site of many of their events. Former Davis Cup captain Alphonso Smith and Philip Morris board chairman Joseph F. Cullman, III, are two typical leaders of the Super Seniors.

The cult of elderly amateurs continues to grow despite gruesome stories about 70-year-olds dropping dead on the court. Like the gunfighters who went out with their boots on, the Super Seniors wouldn't have it any other way.

Neale Fraser

Gardnar Mulloy

Tony Trabert

Lew Hoad

Frank Parker

Bobby Riggs

Jack Kramer

Bill Talbert

Pancho Segura

Frank Sedgman

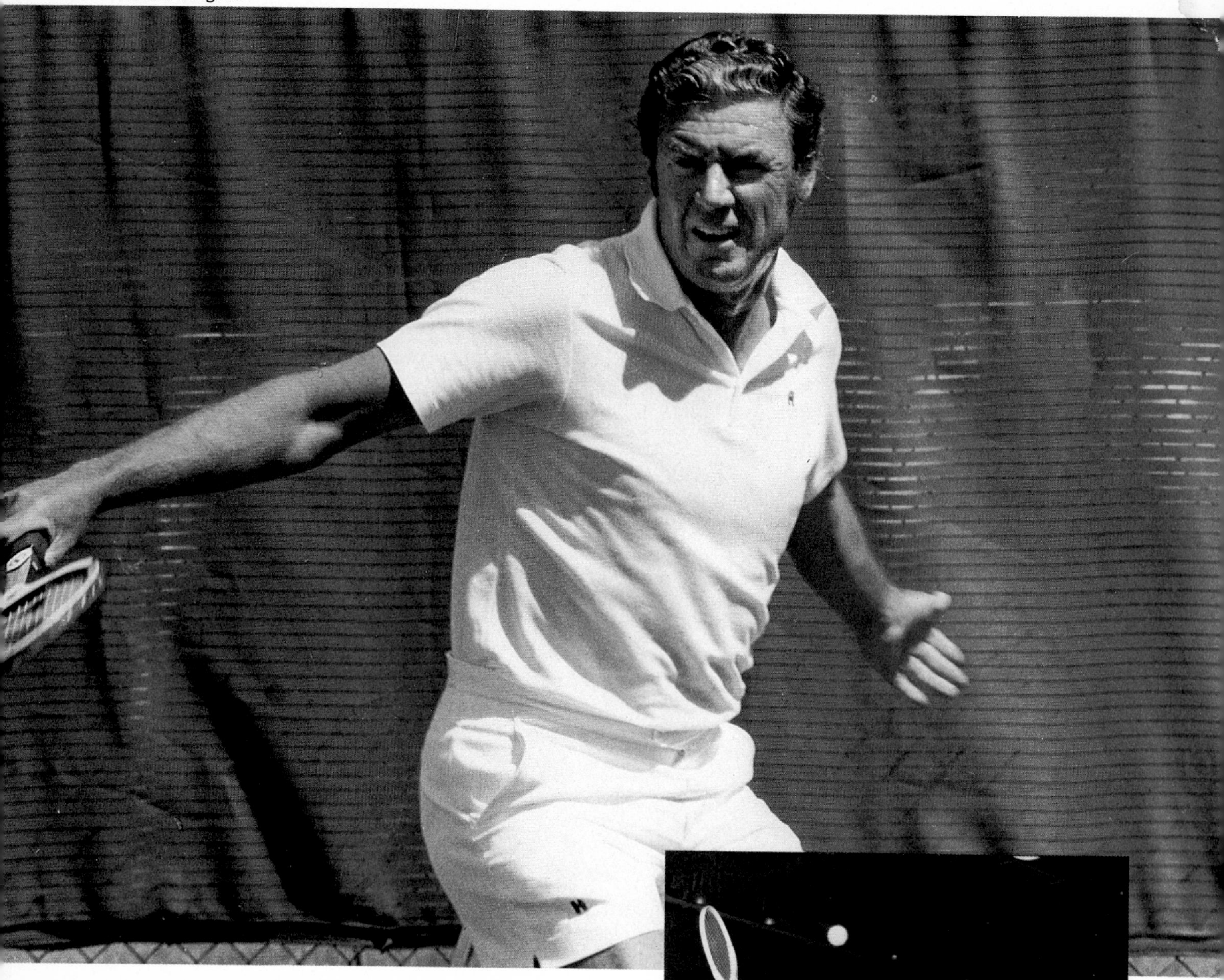

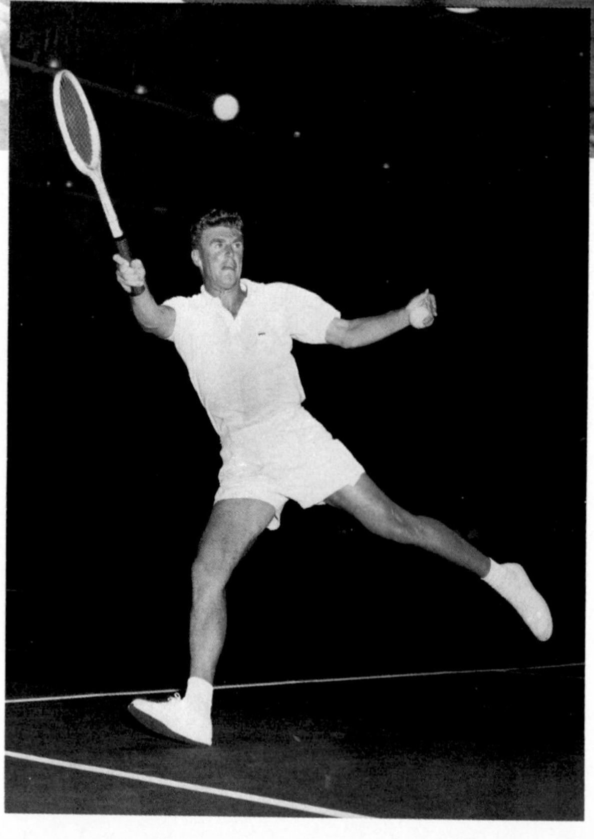

Pancho Gonzalez